THE COLLECTED
PHILOSOPHICAL PAPERS OF
G. E. M. ANSCOMBE

I   From Parmenides to Wittgenstein

THE COLLECTED
PHILOSOPHICAL PAPERS OF
G. E. M. ANSCOMBE

VOLUME ONE

From Parmenides
to Wittgenstein

Basil Blackwell · Oxford

First published in 1981 by
Basil Blackwell Publisher
108 Cowley Road
Oxford OX4 1JF
England

British Library Cataloguing in Publication Data
Anscombe, Gertrude Elizabeth Margaret
The collected philosophical papers of G. E. M. Anscombe.
Vol. 1: From Parmenides to Wittgenstein
1. Philosophy, English – Addresses, essays, lectures
I. Title
192'.08   B1618

ISBN 0-631-12922-7

Typeset in Photon Baskerville

Contents

Acknowledgement   vi

Introduction   vii

PART ONE: The Ancient Greeks

1 Parmenides, Mystery and Contradiction   3

2 The Early Theory of Forms   9

3 The New Theory of Forms   21

4 Understanding Proofs: *Meno*, 85d9 – 86c2, Continued   34

5 Aristotle and the Sea Battle: *De Interpretatione*, Chapter IX   44
  Appendix: A Note on Diodorus Cronus   56

6 The Principle of Individuation   57

7 Thought and Action in Aristotle: What is 'Practical Truth?'   66

PART TWO: Medieval and Modern Philosophers

8 Necessity and Truth   81

9 Hume and Julius Caesar   86

10 "Whatever has a Beginning of Existence must
   have a Cause": Hume's Argument Exposed   93

11 Will and Emotion   100

12 Retractation   108

13 The Question of Linguistic Idealism   112

Index   135

Acknowledgement

I am very grateful to Professor G. H. von Wright for permission to include in this volume the essay 'The Question of Linguistic Idealism' which I contributed to his Festschrift published in *Acta Philosophica Fennica* 28, 1–3 (1976).

Introduction

When I wrote the first essay here reprinted, on Parmenides, I said that no one (so far as I knew) had reasoned thus:

> Only what can be thought can be,
> What is not cannot be thought,
> Therefore what is not cannot be.

I was forgetting the celebrated argument of the Sophists, recorded for us by Plato:

> He who thinks, thinks something,
> He who thinks what is not, thinks nothing,
> Therefore he who thinks what is not is not thinking.

which is certainly an argument for

> What is not cannot be thought

understood in the sense: Whatever is going on, it can't be thinking if, if it *is* thinking, it is thinking what is not.

However, the ground for this is already that what is not *is* nothing, and *this* would lead to "What is not cannot be", unless we think that what is nothing can be. It is more natural to hold that what is nothing cannot be than to go *via* "Only what can be thought can be" in order to reach the conclusion that what is not cannot be. Parmenides himself argues:

> What can be thought can be,
> What is nothing cannot be,
> Therefore whatever can be actually is.
> Therefore whatever can be thought actually is.

All these arguments, except the first one, use as a premise:

> What is not is nothing

and hence do not derive the nothingness of what-is-not from its un-thinkability, but rather its unthinkability either from its nothingness or from its impossibility.

The impossibility of what is not isn't just the impossibility of the pro-position "What is not, is" – i.e. the truth of "What is not cannot be", taken in *sensu composito*. *That* could be swept aside as irrelevant. What is not can't be indeed, but it may come to be, and in this sense what is not is possible. When it *has* come to be, of course it no longer is what is not, so in calling it possible we aren't claiming that "What is not is" is possible. So it can't be shown to be impossible that it should come to be just by pointing to the impossibility that it is. – But this can't be the whole story. That what is not is nothing implies that there isn't anything to come to be. So "What is not can be" taken *in sensu diviso*, namely as: "Concerning what is not, *that* can be" is about nothing at all. If it were about something, then it would be about something that is not, and so there'd be an example of "What is not is" that was true.

If I am right, the ancients never argued from constraints on what could be a thought to restrictions on what could be, but only the other way round.

Only in one place Parmenides states the simple impossibility of the mental condition: "You could not know what is not – for that is not feasible – nor could you express it". Knowledge of what is not is not possible, because knowledge is only of what is, as everybody will agree. That is to say, knowledge that p, when not p, is impossible because if A knows that p, then p. Thus the impossibility of knowledge *here* does not have to be based on the impossibility of the suggested object of knowledge. But for thought the impossibility is based on the impossibility of the suggested object.

"What can be thought and thought's result are the same," he says – and that is nothing but being, or what is. "So anything mortals set up for themselves will be a name – to come to be and pass away, to be and not, to change place and to alter bright colour." – Here the condemnation is not of just anything that may be said about what is, but only of what involves change and non-being. So Parmenides is willing to call his *being* "one" and "changeless" and "continuous" and "like the mass of a well-turned ball", i.e. uniform.

The fact that being is called by other names than "being", such as "one", will lead Plato to argue that *one* and *is* must be different: otherwise we could as well say "one one" as "one is". Similarly the fact that *the one* (which is Parmenides' being) has a name gives Plato his chance to argue that the name is not the same as the one: otherwise we could substitute in "The name is the name of the one" and get "The one is the one of the name". Of course this sentence like "one one" is nonsense, and so he thinks the non-identity of *one* and *being* and the name of the one is proved.

Plato's *ad hominem* arguments made a breach in the wall. There is something besides being, if "one" and "being" both stand for something, but not for the same thing, in the sense that one cannot be replaced by the other; and something besides the one, if the name of the one is not the same as the one itself.

We might get out of the difficulty by saying that "one" and "being" have different senses but still mean the same object. Also, the name of the one has not been proved to be different from the one by non-substitutability of the name "name" and the name "one". Difference of sense for these two names would suffice for non-substitutability in "The name is the name of the one." Similarly, if we have: "The law forbids Jane to marry John" we might replace *either* "Jane" by "his sister" or "John" by "her brother" but if we replace both at once we get the non-sense "The law forbids his sister to marry her brother."

That this *could* make sense if, e.g., "his sister" meant "*that* one's sister" is irrelevant. Just as a product of substitution the sentence is nonsense. But its nonsensicality doesn't show that, in the first sentence and the same sentence with "Jane" replaced by "his sister", "Jane" and "his sister" don't mean the same object.

So Plato's argument fails, unless we may not make the distinction, on Parmenides' behalf, between sense and object meant. But some such distinction is necessary, or else Parmenides would hardly be able to say anything about his one being. In particular, I think I made a false deduction that negative predication was altogether excluded by the objection to not being. It is true that Parmenides tends to avoid it, preferring privative prefixes as in "unchanging"; but he cannot do without it altogether – as when he says that his *being* is not more here, less there. We may count this just as a rejection of "more here, less there". That being fire involves not being earth, being light not being heavy, and so on, brings us into the domain of negative predicates actually holding and so of there *being* such a thing as not-being such and such; and this, it seems, Parmenides really did object to.

If there is any thing that is not Parmenides' *being*, then according to him it is not being, i.e. does not exist, i.e. there isn't any such thing. This suggests that all the different names of things that there are are just different names of that one being; if so there are not many beings after all. If we have two names, phi and xi, such that being phi excludes being xi, then at least one of them cannot be a name of being, because together they will divide being from itself. But there can be nothing against the one being having a multiplicity of names – except that one *name* is not another. But that can be taken as a difference of sense. All names which are names of the same mean the same, and the difference of sense can be taken as a difference in ways of thinking of the one object, not a difference in what is thought of. Sensibly apparent differences of names will be illusory: this is perhaps the hardest consequence.

Parmenides' one being is like the one God, all of whose properties are identical with his being. Or again like Spinoza's one and only substance, except indeed that Parmenides has no room for different modes and affections of the one being.

Plato's escape comes in his *Parmenides* and *Sophist*. These are supposed to be late dialogues, and so the escape was not a presupposition of his start in philosophy or of his earliest theory of forms. He regarded forms as beings, the only beings; but he certainly thought there were many of them, and came to think they differentiated being into parts. He also took it at this late stage that he had to give an account of not being and of the possibility that a thought or proposition, being false, partook of not being, i.e. of 'the other of being'. For this was not the same as what absolutely is not, it itself has being 'running through' it.

One Platonic form was always different from another precisely as an object named by the name of the form. Thus the form of the one is different from the form of being. When we say "one" we are speaking of something other than when we say "is" or "same" or indeed "other".

What Plato has in common with Parmenides is the assumption that a significant term is a name of an object which is either expressed or characterized by the term. For Parmenides, as for Plato, "being" is the only term that expresses being, but for Parmenides such other terms as are not names of nothing are other names of being. What they express is what is true of being, so they characterize it as well as naming it. For Plato significant terms other than "being" are names of beings which are other than being itself but not themselves therefore non-existent, as Parmenides would have it. For being 'runs through' them all. It is thus possible for *the same* not to be other, as well as being other – for it is other than other itself. Parmenides' complaint is verified: being and not being are thought to be the same and not the same.

If we take Parmenides as simply warning us off the path of thinking there are things that do not exist, then he seems no more than good sense. But when we combine this with the idea that *being* is an object, we get his wilder results. However, we should not move slickly here: "being" might be an abstract noun, equivalent to the infinitive "to be". But Parmenides does not treat *to be* as an object, but rather *being*, i.e. something being or some being thing. It is difficult to use the participle in English in the required way, and we might get closer to the sense by saying "what is".

There is a similar difficulty about Parmenides' description of the two paths for thought: "is, and cannot not be", and "is not and needs must not be". In English the lack of a subject may be found disturbing. But the Greek does not need a subject-expression. The subject – he, she, it, or they – is built into the verb, which therefore does not seem incomplete without a separate word for a subject. Therefore it is often translated "It is". But there is no indication in the Greek that "it" is the right subject. Therefore I would rather not give a subject word. "These are the only ways of enquiry for thought: one 'is and cannot not be', . . . the other 'is not, and needs must not be'." That is: Whatever enquiry one is making, one's thoughts can only go two ways, saying 'is, and must be', or 'is not, and can't be'.

The noteworthy thing about this is not so much the ungiven subject, as the combination of "is" with "cannot not be" and of "is not" with "cannot be". This needs argument. We have seen what the argument is: what is not is nothing, and it is not possible for what is nothing to be; and so both whatever can be must be, and what can be thought of must be; for it is the same as what can be.

After Plato, the problem of negation does not seem to have been so prominent; perhaps Plato's rebuttal of Parmenides was accounted sufficient. But the identification of what is true with what must be true remained a focus of discussion. This can be seen from Aristotle's discussion of future contingents and the Master Argument of Diodorus Cronus. It appears again in Aquinas' discussion of divine knowledge of the future. Aristotle and his greatest scholastic follower are marked by an indeterminism about such future events as do not have necessitating causes already in the present: this stance involves them in logical problems.

The assumption common to Plato and Parmenides is an ancestor of much philosophical theorizing and perplexity. In Aristotle its descendant is the theory of substance and the inherence in substances of individualized forms of properties and relations of various kinds. In Descartes it is reflected in the assertion that the descriptive terms which we use to construct even false pictures of the world must themselves stand for realities – even if the pictures are of nothing, the colours in which they are painted are real. In Hume there is the assumption that 'an object' corresponds to a term, even such a term as "a cause" as it occurs in "A beginning of existence must have a cause." And he is also convinced that what can be lacking in a thought can be lacking to the reality that the thought is of. Brentano thinks that the mere predicative connection of terms is an 'acknowledgement' (*Anerkennung*): he apparently forgets at this point both that predication need not be assertion and that assertions may not be true. He would have done better to say, with Wittgenstein in the *Tractatus Logico-Philosophicus*, that the proposition *shows* how things are *if* it is true, and *says* that that is how they are (whether it is asserted or not). Wittgenstein himself in the *Tractatus* has language pinned to reality by its (postulated) simple names, which mean simple objects.

It was left to the moderns to deduce what could be from what could hold of thought, as we see Hume to have done. This trend is still strong. But the ancients had the better approach, arguing only that a thought was impossible because the thing was impossible, or, as the *Tractatus* puts it. "Was man nicht denken kann, das kann man nicht denken": an *impossible* thought is an impossible *thought*.

At the present day we are often perplexed with enquiries about what makes true, or what something's being thus or so *consists in*; and the answer to this is thought to be an explanation of meaning. If there is no external answer, we are apparently committed to a kind of idealism.

Whitehead's remark about Plato might, somewhat narrowly, be applied to his great predecessor:

Subsequent philosophy is footnotes on Parmenides.

Part One

The Ancient Greeks

1 Parmenides, Mystery and Contradiction

Parmenides' argument runs:

> It is the same thing that can be thought and can be
> What is not can't be
> ∴ What is not can't be thought

This is valid only if the second premise is taken *in sensu diviso*. But it has no credibility except *in sensu composito*. The conclusion is also incredible.

The first premise is false if *either* that can be thought which cannot be *or* that can be which cannot be thought; though only the former is relevant to Parmenides' argument. Pictures of impossible states of affairs seem to favour the former. Descartes would say these don't give us clear and distinct ideas. Where the picture can be grasped without oscillation of attention that is difficult to substantiate. The impossibility of thinking that there is such a thing as the picture presents cannot, of course, be offered as proof that the idea is not clear and distinct. − But it must be granted that these are out-of-the-way cases. Besides, Parmenides might be taken to mean: the impossible can't be clearly conceived *to be*.

He reaches a conclusion as to what cannot be thought. From this conclusion or just from the second premise he is able further to infer:

(1) A false thought is impossible
(2) A negative thought is impossible
(3) Change is impossible
(4) Past and future, and so, we may add, past and future tensed thoughts, are impossible
(5) Differentiation is impossible.

He might support the second premise taken *in sensu diviso*:

> Concerning that which is not, it holds that *that* cannot be,

saying: What have you mentioned? Nothing at all. And that's my point! Admittedly the same holds of the conclusion:

> Concerning that which is not, it holds that *that* cannot be thought.

But this is the difficulty any philosopher is in, rejecting, by reasoning, an essentially incoherent thought. He has to formulate it somehow in order to show it up as incoherent.

From *Proceedings of the Aristotelian Society* (1969).

But we may reply: We didn't purport to mention anything when we said "Concerning what is not." Your premise comes to this:

$$(F)(x) \sim F\ x \longrightarrow Nec \sim Fx$$

or $$\sim p \longrightarrow Nec \sim p$$

and that is not credible; nor can you appeal to your rejection of negatives to protest against this way of putting the premise, for that rejection is based on the conclusion of just this argument.

He might reply in turn: What do you mean, you didn't purport to *mention* anything? Take the first symbolic formulation: you may not have mentioned non-existence, or the non-existent as such, as appears to be done in:

Concerning the non-existent it holds that *that* can't be,

but you mentioned properties and objects. Can you allow your variable F to range over non-existent as well as existent properties, any more than your variable *x* to range over non-existent as well as existent objects? If *not*, then

$$(\exists F)\ (x) \sim Fx$$

is impossible. So we have

$$Nec \sim(\exists F)\ (x) \sim Fx$$

and therefore

$$Nec\ (F)\ (\exists x)\ Fx$$

Now since, if negation is admissible, we can always form a negative predicate, it will follow from this that no properties are universal, not even self-identity. Therefore your argument commits you to the belief, e.g. that there are things that aren't identical with themselves. Or, to put the same point without mentioning negation, there are things that are different from themselves.

Would you rather say – he might go on – that the existence of properties is something *other* than their holding of something? Only so, it seems, can there be a property which nothing has. Will you say, then, that though you can speak of non-existent objects, i.e. of there not being any objects of certain kinds, you cannot speak of non-existent properties? Then all properties exist, including the most self-contradictory ones? Self-contradiction in what exists is just what I set out to avoid, and you pretended that I *could* do that without accepting the conclusion "What is not cannot be thought." But your insistence that what is not can be has landed you in self-contradiction after all. So pay that price, or go along with me.

And – he might continue – were you not labouring under an illusion, i.e. failing to produce real thoughts, in fancying you could use these techniques of a later time to show that my thought was fallacious? For I perceive that your thinkers introduce as existent a null class, as the class with no members, e.g. the class of things with such and such contradictory properties. So they admit contradictory properties, i.e. use them to determine a class, and stop short if anywhere only at paradoxical ones, which nevertheless they know cannot be avoided as a possibility in natural languages.

To this we can reply: it is false that one mentions either properties or objects when one uses the quantifiers binding property variables and object variables; though it has to be granted that some authors, such as Quine, are accustomed to speak of the reference of variables. But if this is given up, as it ought to be, Parmenides is deprived of his claim that we are committed to self-contradiction in existence just because we are willing to use a self-contradictory predicate – e.g. in the sentence saying that nothing has a self-contradictory predicate true of it – so that our property-variable is admitted to range over self-contradictory properties.

So farewell Parmenides.

That other arm of his first premise, which he does not in fact use, remains tantalizing. What he used was 'Only that can be thought, which can be'; the other arm of his premise is 'Only that can be, which can be thought'.

We might call this arm of the premise the 'No Mystery' arm. If some way of characterizing what can be thought could be found, then if this proposition is true, there's a quick way of excluding mysteries.

But here we badly need to distinguish the different things that may be meant by the proposition "It is the same thing that can be thought and can be." To take first the arm Parmenides actually used, it seems it might mean:

    (1) Only what can exist can be thought of
    (2) Only what can exist can be thought to exist
    (3) Only what can be the case can be thought to be the case
    (4) Only what can be the case can be thought of.

On any of these interpretations Parmenides' own argument is vitiated by the requirement of the argument that the second premise be taken *in sensu diviso*, in which it isn't credible. i.e., whether we interpret the premise as saying:

What doesn't exist can't exist

or as:

What isn't the case can't be the case

the proposition is not credible. Thus it wasn't necessary to distinguish the various things Parmenides' "be" and "think" might mean in considering his actual argument, except that it might make a difference to our estimate of the first premise.

"Only what can exist, or can be the case, can be thought *of*" seems refuted by the argument from the impossible pictures.

"Only what can be the case can be thought to be the case" is evidently false
– if we aren't very restrictive on what we call thinking something.

"Only what can exist can be thought to exist" is false for the same reason.

However the impossible pictures show that something can be conceived
which, just *as* it is conceived and understood, can't be conceived to exist. And
what may be true is that:

Only what can be the case can, without misunderstanding, logical error,
or confusion, be thought to be the case

and:

Only what can exist can, without misunderstanding, logical error or confusion, be thought to exist.

And this proposition is perhaps acceptable.

But now let's try the other arm, the 'No Mystery' arm:

Only what can be thought can be.

The difference between the various interpretations becomes important:

(1) Only what can be thought of can exist
(2) Only what can be thought to exist can exist
(3) Only what can be thought to be the case can be the case
(4) Only what can be thought of can be the case.

If the thesis is going to be used in an argument something like
Parmenides', we shall have a second premise (what is in fact Parmenides'
conclusion):

> What is not
> or is not the case $\left\{\text{can't}\right\}$ be thought of
> or be thought to be the case

yielding as conclusion the Parmenidean premise "What is not (or is not the
case) can't be (or be the case)".

This however is not a path anyone has taken so far as I know, though one
might, if reading inattentively, think that Parmenides did argue like that.

What people have done is to try some other subject in the second premise,
i.e. not "What is not", as subject for "can't be thought".

Here are some resulting arguments if we try this task:

(1) Only what can be thought of can be
   A seventh regular solid can't be thought of
   ∴ A seventh regular solid can't be
(2) Only what can be thought to be the case can be the case
   The contradictory can't be thought to be the case
   ∴ The contradictory can't be the case
(3) Only what can be thought to be the case can be the case

The unverifiable-in-principle can't be thought to be the case
∴ The unverifiable-in-principle can't be the case

Presented with the first argument, one's hackles rise. If the only reason for saying a seventh regular solid can't be is that it can't be thought of, then perhaps it's just that we can't manage the thought. And in a way, of course, it can be thought of.

The second argument, about the contradictory, meets the difficulty that the contradictory *can* be thought to be the case – and if we put in "wittingly" the first premise with "wittingly" inserted becomes totally doubtful. For presumably it means:

Only what can be thought to be the case by someone who has in mind all the implications of what he thinks, can be the case.

But since $p \longrightarrow p \lor q$, it is impossible for someone to have in mind all the implications of anything at all. So if the premise were true, nothing could be the case.

But what are we to make of this first premise anyway?

It appears to draw attention to the possibilities for thought – and who knows what they are? If I say I can think something, what of it? If I say I can't, does that mean I can't manage to do what I do in the other case? Again, what of it?

Let us try the negation of the proposition:

(A) There may be what can't be thought.
(Not: what one can't invest with the feeling of having thought it, but what eludes explanation, what remains enigmatic.)

At first sight one might think one could disprove this by arguing that if it is a thought, then its content is contradicted by the fact that it is a thought. I can't think of anything I can't think of. But this is wrong. For in thinking (A) one is not purporting to think the unthinkable, any more than, in thinking that there is something one isn't thinking of, one is purporting to think of something one isn't thinking of.

However, 'was ich nicht weiß, macht mich nich heiß'. If the thought "Something that can't be thought may be" *isn't yet* the thought of, as we say, anything in particular, we've no need to worry. True: but wouldn't it be satisfactory if we could refute

There may be what can't be thought

or:

Something may be which can't be grasped in thought?

The idea has at any rate had a strong appeal. For then no one could have any right to produce a *particular* sentence and say: this is true, but what it says is irreducibly enigmatic. Of course if the sentence is mere abracadabra no one will take any notice. But suppose the sentence is not abracadabra but yet there are difficulties about claiming an unexceptionable sense for it? If that is the situation, can we dismiss the possibility that this enigmatic sense is a truth?

If we could prove Parmenides' principle, or rather the arm of it that he did not use, we might say:

Since the sentence *cannot* be taken as expressing a clear thought – i.e. a thought which is clearly free from contradiction or other conceptual disorder – therefore it doesn't say anything, and therefore not anything true. And that would be very agreeable. We could perhaps become quite satisfied that a sentence was in that sense irreducibly enigmatic – and so we could convince ourselves we had the right to dismiss it.

This suggests as the sense of "can be grasped in thought"; "can be presented in a sentence which can be seen to have an unexceptionable non-contradictory sense".

A form of: whatever can be said at all can be said clearly.

Someone who thought this *might* think "There may be the inexpressible." And so in that sense think "There may be what can't be thought". – But he wouldn't be exercised by any definite claimant to be that which can't be grasped in thought. *Mystery* would be illusion – either the thought expressing something mysterious could be clarified, and then no mystery, or the impossibility of clearing it up would show it was really a non-thought.

The trouble is, there doesn't seem to be any ground for holding this position. It is a sort of prejudice.

2   The Early Theory of Forms

There is a philosophic theory which is *accepted as certain* by the participants in the discussion in the *Phaedo*. This is the theory of forms or types (see 92d and 100c). I use the word "type" on purpose, unfamiliar as it is in this context. Nowadays when talking about words or letters people distinguish between 'types' and 'tokens'; there may be 100 tokens of the type letter e on a page, but e itself is just one letter. That gives one some conception of a Platonic form. The theory is as follows:

(1) We ordinarily assume a single kind or type in connection with any plurality to which we apply a common name F (*Republic*, 596a).

(2) This single type F, however, is different from the many Fs, to which the common name F is applied (*Phaedo*, 74a, c). It is not to be identified as those things, nor are any of those things to be identified with it (*Republic*, 476c).

(3) The many Fs resemble, or are copies of the single type F (*Republic*, 402, 472, 484, 500, 501, 510, 520, 540; *Phaedrus*, 250, 251).

So much is regarded as obvious. To this we may add the following, which are either supplementations to (1), (2), (3) from other dialogues groupable with the *Phaedo*, or are expressly argued for in the *Phaedo*:

(4) It is characteristically human to understand according to such single types (*Phaedrus*, 249b); each is a unitary object derived by contraction to a single thing from a multitude of perceptions by the power of reason (*Phaedrus*, 249b–c).

(5) This process of contracting into one (*Phaedrus*) or of acquiring knowledge of F itself by seeing F sticks and F stones – e.g. of *equal* by seeing equal sticks and equal stones (*Phaedo*, 74a–b) – is a process of being reminded by the many Fs of the type, F itself, with which the mind has been acquainted in previous existence (*Phaedrus*, 249c; *Phaedo*, 74d–75a).

(6) The mind is reminded of the type F by perceiving Fs because of their resemblance to the type F itself (*Phaedo*, 74–5).

(7) This resemblance is imperfect inasmuch as it often happens that a particular F thing – i.e. thing we call F – is also somehow not F. This affords a further proof that no particular F is to be identified with the type F: for that, F itself, cannot possibly fail to be F (*Phaedo*, 74–5).

(8) The relation of other Fs to the kind or type, that they *have* it (*Republic*, 597c), or participate in it (*Phaedo*, 101c), is quite obscure and naming it as *having* or *participation* is not meant to be informative. Plato in the *Parmenides* raised the question of how this 'participation' or 'sharing' worked – does something sharing in F have the whole of F or part of it? Is participation

---

This paper has not previously been published.

resemblance? (*Parmenides*, 132–3) The question is not solved by Socrates in *Parmenides*.

(9) There are no two distinct types F, where Fs are a plurality all called by the same name F, such that the many Fs participate in both, or either (*Republic*, 597c).

(10) The type F, F itself or F-ness (the abstract form occurs, though not as often as the concrete "F itself") is F. Indeed it is the only thing that *is*, as opposed to participating in, F (*Republic*, 597c).

(11) The type F is eternal, simple and changeless (*Phaedo*, 78d).

(12) The type F is thus non-temporal and not to be found in any place in heaven or earth. In the *Phaedrus* Plato locates these objects *beyond* the heavens: but this is in a passage declaredly figurative as far as concerns the character of the soul, which comes to this place beyond the heavens to see the types: and so the localization itself may well be figurative. "A place beyond the heavens" might have the same ring as "Somewhere outside space" would for us (*Phaedrus*, 247c–e).

Some people would add to this list of conceptions determining what Plato meant by a form, that there is a form wherever there is a set of resembling objects. So far as I know Plato does not use this conception. Since he thinks that our *souls* resemble the divine and the types to a certain extent, it is not a very probable foundation for the theory. It is mentioned in the *Parmenides*; Parmenides introduces it (*Parmenides*, 132 d–e), saying "Isn't it very necessary that *resembling* things should participate in a single type?" and Socrates acquiesces. Socrates has just suggested that participation may *be* resemblance; and certainly in the *Phaedo* and elsewhere he regarded the many Fs as resemblances of the F itself, the type or form F. His acquiescence in Parmenides' suggestion is therefore disastrous; if all resembling things are of a separately existing type, and all particular Fs *resemble* the type F, then all particular Fs plus the type F must be of a further distinct type – and so we are in for a vicious infinite regress. But I do not know of any other place where it is suggested – as it seems to be in this place in the *Parmenides* – that *some* similar things, *qua* similar, must all be of one type F and other similar things of one type G and so on. That is, forms are not elsewhere introduced as different similarities – students of modern philosophy in the British Empiricist tradition need warning *against* this approach. Thus it looks as if Socrates ought to have repudiated the 'great necessity' of this principle, except in the sense that similar things share in the form 'similarity'. Or (as he says earlier (129d5)), echoing the *Phaedo* doctrine, similars are similar *by* similarity and *not by anything else* at all.

Not that in this way he can avoid all contradictions. For there is another such infinite regress of types previously extracted by Parmenides from premises, which he certainly does not foist on Socrates as I suggest he foists on him the necessity for sets of resembling objects to be of one type. If one grasps a type F in connection with the many Fs, then, if F itself *is* F, one will grasp a second type in connection with the many Fs taken together with F itself. And so on *ad infinitum*. If "F" should actually *be* "similar" the argument will of course apply to it as to any other form: but Socrates need not have admitted attack by two *separate* infinite regress arguments.

It is clear that in order to get out of this difficulty it would be necessary to develop something already hinted at in the *Republic*, namely that the ways in which the type F is F and in which a particular F is F are too different to allow us to put F itself and the many Fs together into a plurality. Just as we should not say that there were three beds in a room if there were an ordinary bed there and also a picture showing two beds, so we can't say that an ordinary bed and the bed itself make two beds. This does not mean a retreat from Self-Predication, it rather develops the suggestion of the Republic that the bed itself alone is *what is a bed* (597c).

The present-day theoretical concept most like a Platonic form, or type as I have called it, is the concept of a class. This will surprise only those who suppose that a class *is* its members, that there is nothing to it but those objects which are its members. Or again, that a class is composed of its members as a wall is composed of bricks. It is this comforting picture that gives the concept of 'class' as used among philosophers the deceptive air of being both an impeccable logical notion and a down-to-earth sort of conception with no 'metaphysics' about it. The class of people in this room at present is simply . . . and now I give a list. One should realize that this is a total misconception about classes when one encounters the null class; for in the sense in which a class or set simply *is* that lot of objects, an empty class does not exist, just because it has no members. But for purposes of logic the null class is indispensable.

Or take the opening of Quine's *Set Theory and its Logic*:

> We can say that a class is any aggregate, any collection, any combination of objects of any sort; if this helps, well and good. But even this will be less help than hindrance unless we keep clearly in mind that the aggregating or collecting or combining here is to connote no actual displacement of the objects, and further that the aggregation or collection or combination of say seven given pairs of shoes is not to be identified with the aggregation or collection or combination of those fourteen shoes, nor with that of the twenty-eight soles and uppers. In short, a class may be thought of as an aggregate or collection or combination of objects just so long as 'aggregate' or 'collection' or 'combination' is understood strictly in the sense of 'class'.[1]

A class in modern logic is thus something *besides* the things of which a certain predicate holds, or, as Plato would say, *besides* the things to which we apply the same name. This is the doctrine of *separate existence* which is the great rock of offence in the Platonic Theory of Forms.

It might seem that Plato's forms differed from classes by the Law of Extensionality which applies to classes: classes which have the same members are

---

[1] *Set Theory and its Logic* (Cambridge, Mass., 1963), p. 1.

the same. Surely, we may say, forms participated in by the same objects are not *thereby* the same?

But we must scrutinize the Law of Extensionality a little more closely. What classes *do* have the same members? Since a class is not the same thing as its members taken collectively – is not just *those objects* but something besides – it can matter *how you take* those objects. And it *does* matter. This shoe is *not* a member of the class one of whose members is the pair to which this shoe belongs. The class of the fourteen shoes and the class of the seven pairs are different classes with different members. Now Plato explained a type as what we customarily assume for each plurality to which we apply the same name; and he argued that there were never *two* types for such a plurality to be of. So here again his concept of a type or form is noticeably similar to the modern logician's notion of a class. There are indeed several different class-concepts for any class; it does not matter how you characterize a class so long as your characterizations apply to just the same things as members of the class. However, it does not look as if Plato's conception of definition was other than extensional – in the *Meno* Socrates simply looks around for a definition of colour that will apply to all colour and in the *Sophist* Plato propounds various definitions of the Sophist which do not supplant one another.

The puzzle about participation in a form recurs about membership of a class. This relation is dark because as we have seen the members do not *constitute* a class. 'Membership' of a class and 'participation' in a Platonic kind might be called the same notion, which no one has been able to explicate and which people take as a rock-bottom notion – but which surely does need explication if the class, type or form, is something separate.

This resemblance of the notion of a class to that of a Platonic Form is recognized by those who have studied the matter. In Anders Wedberg's wonderfully valuable book *Plato's Philosophy of Mathematics*[2] it is remarked upon; Wedberg notices that the Law of Extensionality may well apply to forms so that that does not differentiate them from classes. He says, however, that classes are collections and forms are not; this is a failure to notice that classes are only collections "if", as Quine says, "you understand 'collection' as equivalent to 'class'", i.e. in just as special a way.

Still it would be wrong to think that there is no difference between Platonic forms and classes, or that this is not *in part* connected with the extensional conception of classes. For one thing Plato does not speak, so far as I know, of forms in which nothing participates; so, just as the number o does not occur in his mathematics, no analogue of the null class occurs in his philosophy. This is a rather greater degree of what some call "metaphysicality" on the part of the moderns.

There is this further point in favour of the feeling that the *extensionality* of class concepts makes them contrast with Platonic forms. Plato would not have forms *red square* or *white man*; but the *meet* of the class of red things and of squares is itself a class. Similarly for the *join* of two classes: we have the

[2] Stockholm, 1955.

class of things that are either men or horses, but "either a man or a horse" would not be a designation of a distinct form. A thing isn't either-a-horse-or-a-man, it's either a horse or a man! This attempt to say something breaks down – which has made one think it unsayable – but perhaps we *could* say it like this: A thing isn't, e.g., either-a-horse-or-a-man, it either *is a horse* or *is a man*. The contrast will not impress someone used to doing things as they are done in logic nowadays; but, whether there is anything in it or not, it has about it a strong flavour of Greek philosophy about forms, predicates and being.

Again, Plato would never – we may surely say with safety – give a form by enumerating the things that participated in it. This is one standard way of giving a class.

The similarity, however, especially in the great rock of offence, is fairly striking. The rock of offence is that a form is something 'besides' the particular things that have it; that is the same as the doctrine of 'separate existence'. It was this doctrine that offended Aristotle, who dwelt obsessively on the theory of forms and is apt to be found having a bang at it in every context: we may say the theory of forms was to him what private ostensive definition was to Wittgenstein. "Plato is our friend but truth is dearer", he said. Echoing this there is a famous remark of Tarski's "Inimicus Plato sed magis inimica falsitas" – "We don't like Plato but falsehood is worse": an acknowledgement of the common rock of offence.

But the dislike of Plato is probably connected not just with the rock of offence which the theory of classes avoids as little as the theory of forms, but with further aspects of the theory of forms which are foreign to the theory of classes.

First, the theory of forms is a theory of characteristically human understanding, as the theory of classes is not. Second, it is a theory of what are the true objects of knowledge; it is not professed in set-theory that sets are the only true and truly knowable objects. Third, the forms are supposed to have a pure and divine sort of existence; nothing like that holds of classes. Again, it is not heard of that, in general, members of classes resemble them – let alone that the class of Fs is a kind of *cause* of an F's being F. (Here I anticipate a doctrine of the *Phaedo* which will get closer discussion.) Finally, many class-concepts are concepts of relation to individuals. Assuming Asclepius to have existed, the descendants of Asclepius, for example, would form a class, but it would probably be quite foreign to Plato to admit a form in connection with Asclepiads. Of course it is difficult to see why this plurality with a common name should *not* involve us in the assumption of a form: but it seems clear that this connection with an individual would be a *contamination* from Plato's point of view, incompatible with that 'pure and divine' existence appropriate to the forms. Relations are indeed a difficulty for the theory of forms, a difficulty with which Parmenides presents Socrates: the master as such, he suggests, will be *of* the slave as such, or the type: master, of the type: slave, and not of any individual slave. This leads to the conclusion that the world of forms is quite dissociated from our world, and the gods, who have knowledge which is *knowledge itself*, can neither know nor govern our affairs. The conclusion is not satisfactory to Socrates but he cannot solve the problem.

In contrasting forms and classes I mentioned one point in the doctrine of forms which I did not put into my list (1)–(11): that a form F is a *cause* of F things being or becoming. I left this out because it is not part of the doctrine of forms that is accepted as obviously right, as the best possible assumption one can make; nor is it an amplification that can readily be supplied. It is introduced in a rather special way, without *argument* but with a good deal of *fuss*: Socrates says that in raising a certain doubt about the immortality of the soul Cebes is involving him in a general enquiry about generation and corruption. He then gives us a bit of autobiography, telling how as a young man he was occupied with natural-scientific questions about the causes of things, such as how flesh grows:

> It's a very queer thing,
> As queer as can be,
> That whatever Miss T. eats,
> Turns into Miss T.

After a lot of thought he came to the conclusion that he did not at all understand certain seemingly obvious statements about how things come about. He gives as examples that he did not understand how it is that:

(1) Flesh accrues to flesh out of food through eating and drinking.
(2) One man is taller than another by a head.
(3) Ten exceeds eight by two.
(4) The addition of one to one makes two.
(5) The division of one makes two.

While in this perplexity, he heard that the philosopher Anaxagoras held that mind was the cause of everything, and he thought that sounded splendid and would mean that Anaxagoras explained everything in terms of what was best. However, Anaxagoras' book did nothing of the sort. This remained Socrates' desire, but, in default of supplying this kind of explanation, he must he says for the present adopt another. Using his assumption, which everybody grants him, that the forms exist, the most powerful explanatory assumption that he can make is that, if something other than the form F is or comes to be F, it is or comes to be F *by* the form F, or, an equivalent formulation, by participation in the form F. This is certainly an addition to the theory as I have so far sketched it. That said that particular Fs had, or participated in, F itself, but not that this was a *cause* of their being F.

Socrates does not intend this to exclude other types of causality. He still wants an explanation in terms of 'the best'; and he calls explanations like 'food', the addition of one to one, division, just too difficult for him – but he does not imply that they are false.

With hindsight we can see here the first adumbrations of the various kinds of cause described by Aristotle. The explanation in terms of the best that Socrates hankers after is something like an explanation in terms of final causality; food and the two ones in two are material causes; eating, drinking, digestion, addition and division might be efficient causes; and the sort of cause which Socrates offers as the best he can do for the time being is what Aristotle called the *formal* cause. 'By a head' and 'by two' in "taller by a head" and "greater by two" do not have an analogue that I know of in any causal concept.

We come now to the most obscure passage in the *Phaedo*. The dialogue has regularly spoken of *assuming* – the Greek word is the verb from which 'hypothesis' comes – the existence of the forms and the hypothesis of the forms. This however does not imply any uncertainty; the participants are *very* sure of this doctrine and its corollary, the pre-existence of the soul. Now however Socrates speaks of assuming the strongest account available to him – in default of an explanation in terms of good and mind; and in relation to *this* hypothesis the word begins to get a more technical sense, in which an hypothesis *needs to be based on something else* before it can be finally accepted.

This "strongest available hypothesis" is that, if something other than the beautiful itself is beautiful, then it is beautiful *through* the beautiful itself or *because* it participates in that.

Socrates says he doesn't know how this works – whether by presence of the form or communion in it – but the *safest* thing to say about causes is:

What makes beautiful is the beautiful
What makes bigger is bigness
What makes smaller is smallness
What makes ten more than eight is multitude
What makes two when one is added to one is the Dyad – i.e. Two itself
Whatever is to be one will be one by the Monad – i.e. *One* itself.

Socrates next says that if one is to follow him one must hang on to that safe point in the hypothesis, and simply answer like that if asked about causes. But if anyone hangs on to the hypothesis itself, one must make no answer till one has tested it for consistency. If however one is asked to give an *account* of that hypothesis itself one must assume higher hypotheses until one comes to something adequate. Above all one must not confuse principles and their consequences like the disputatious Sophists. This last remark is the one thing that is clear about this difficult passage; and it shows Plato up as having a very screwy idea of reasoning. For there is nothing wrong with mixing up premises and conclusions derived from them so as to derive fresh conclusions. Consider, if a.b. → c and c.d. → e one can put a.b.d. → e. Take a particular case of this συνθετικον θεωρημα, where d = a: we have a.b → c and a.c → e. So we can put a.b → e. This quite valid procedure Plato had apparently decided was what was wrong with the arguments of some of the Sophists. These people constructed arguments which, as Mrs Kneale put it in the

Development of Logic,[3] "would not deceive a child" – as far as *believing* the argument goes, of course! But it is one thing to see that an argument must be wrong, another to say accurately what was wrong with it. Here we have Plato making a very general boss shot at characterizing sophists' fallacies.

The rest of the passage is so obscure that many translators render the first occurrence of one and the same verb ἐχεσθαι "hang on to" and the next occurrence, in the next line, "attack" – which is intolerably harsh. Nobody makes such shifts to some quite contrary sense a verb may be capable of, unless in a very pointed manner. It must mean "hang on to" both times.

The puzzle is that evidently the person who is hanging on to the hypothesis itself is doing something different from the person who is hanging on to the safe point about it. Most translators take "the safe thing about the hypothesis" – literally "the safe of the hypothesis" – to mean the safety of the hypothesis, i.e. the safe hypothesis itself. However, the reading "what is safe about the hypothesis" appears to me a very possible way of taking the Greek as Greek, and the only way of making sense of the passage.

This safe thing was of course the thing mentioned as "safe" before, but just in the particular instance that occurs in this paragraph: if there is a result two when one is added to one, or *if* anything is to be one, in every case this is *through* the form.

Then what is the hypothesis as opposed to this 'safe thing about it' – for only *that* has so far been introduced expressly as an hypothesis?

I can see no answer but that the hypothesis is: that *there is* a result two; or more precisely that one being added to one, or divided, it comes about that there are two; the text does not say this doesn't happen, but that the only cause one will be confident in giving will not be *addition*, or *division*. That is the result Socrates arrived at when he puzzled about how the addition of one to one should bring it about that *there are two*. And this is a genuine difficulty. Of course you can add one egg to another egg *in a basket* and then where you had *one egg in a basket*, by the approach of one – other – egg you have *two eggs in a basket*. But if you just say one and one are two and mean the number one, not one *of* anything, then isn't it nonsense? Or if you mean one and one of anything you had, they were already two before, weren't they? No need to add them or bring them together. Does "one" mean the same both times? If so why not say the moon and the moon make two? Does "one" mean something different in its two occurrences? If so, what? And how is the *opposite* process of separation *also* supposed to make two? Readers of Frege's *Foundations of Arithmetic* will recognize the source of my duplication of Socrates' difficulty.

In further defence of my interpretation, I appeal to two sources of help. One is the *Republic* which has a passage so closely similar to the *Phaedo* passage in certain points that it seems certain they relate to the same matter. The other is some very pertinent information given by Aristotle in *Metaphysics* XIII about Plato's teachings – which may of course be rather developed in

[3] W. C. & M. Kneale, *The Development of Logic* (Oxford, 1962), p. 13.

comparison with what we have in the *Phaedo* and the *Republic*; but it seems to cast a great deal of light on these if we see in them the germ of what Aristotle gives an account of.

Aristotle says that Plato distinguished between two sorts of numbers. First, 'mathematical' numbers, each of which had many instances and which were 'combinable' and composed of exactly similar units. Plato says mathematicians are concerned with such numbers as these at *Republic*, 526: "If someone were to ask them: what sort of numbers are you talking about, which contain *one* as you conceive it, every single one equal to every one, not differing in the least, containing no parts? how would they answer? . . . that they are speaking of things which can only be grasped in thought." The other sort were the numbers which were forms: there was only one of each of these and they were uncombinable and the units of which any one was composed were all unlike one another and uncombinable. These would be '*the* monad, *the* dyad' of which Plato speaks in the *Phaedo*.

Combinability and uncombinability are readily explained. For example, if in a more modern vein we explain the number two as the class of couples, then any member of any couple will combine with any other member of any couple to make a couple and a set which is the join of one couple and another non-overlapping couple will be a set of four. But if you follow someone like von Neumann and define 0 as the null class and each number as the class whose members are its predecessors, you get:

0 The null class
1 The class whose only member is the null class
2 The class whose only members are: the null class and the class whose only member is the null class

or

0 The null class
1 The class whose only member is 0
2 The class whose only members are 0 and 1, etc.

Now you cannot combine the members of *these* classes in the following sense. If you try thinking of the addition of two and three as a matter of combining the members of the classes two and three you will be trying to combine:

2 The null class
The class whose only member is the null class

with

3 The null class
The class whose only member is the null class
The class whose only members are the null class and the class whose only member is the null class

And that is like combining (A and B) with (A and B and C) – at any rate you won't get five that way! *We* indeed shouldn't much object to speaking of combining AB and ABC, the result will only be ABC still; but firstly the ancients would probably have objected, and secondly, even if they would not, at any rate combining here is not that join of non-overlapping sets which yields a set of the appropriate number.

If we read *Phaedo*, 101c–e and *Republic*, 510b–11c we get a strong impression that they relate to the same matters.

Putting the two passages together we get as Plato's doctrine:

(1) Ordinary mathematics postulates numbers (e.g. one and two), it postulates odd and even, figures, angles and so on (*Phaedo* and *Republic*). Perhaps we may say it postulates that two is generated (*Phaedo*). At any rate it postulates being one and becoming two (*Phaedo*) and geometrical shapes (*Republic*). The development of the propositions of arithmetic and the theorems of geometry goes forwards from these postulates or hypotheses.

(2) It is essential to mathematics to use drawings and physical objects; these are mere images for what the mathematician is after: he uses them to try and see the forms, which, however we learn in the next book of the Republic can only really be seen by pure intelligence engaged in dialectic (*Republic*, 533c-d).

(3) The forms are *not* the postulated numbers, angles, figures, etc. but are the causes of these (*Phaedo*) if these exist.

I say "if they exist", because they are only the hypotheses that Plato is speaking of, and he says that the safe thing about the hypothesis – and hence presumably the only safe thing about it – is that the dyad is the cause of there coming to be two, etc.; and also speaks of testing the hypothesis, if anyone holds fast to it, by seeing if it is consistent: thus it appears that he does not regard the hypothesis itself as certain, but only thinks it certain that if these postulated numbers, etc., exist, the forms are their causes.

(4) The philosopher who follows Socrates will react to the postulation of numbers, angles, figures, etc., by seeing if they are consistent notions; i.e. by seeing if he can derive a contradiction from these hypotheses (*Phaedo*).

Plato seems to leave it an open question whether such a contradiction can be derived or not. Ordinary mathematical reasonings to propositions of arithmetic and theorems of geometry seem to be admitted as consistent (533c5) but, I suggest, that is not the only question at issue. There seem to be strong hints that there are frightful difficulties about the postulated numbers and figures. For example, the mathematician, who is trying to glimpse the square as such (*Republic*, 511a1) and so presumably is also trying to glimpse, e.g., the monad and the dyad of the *Phaedo*, says indignantly that he is not talking about visible bodies that have numbers (*Republic*, 525d8): no, he is talking about numbers, in which each *one* is exactly the same as *any other* one (526a2). There are thus several *ones* in any of his numbers. Since there can be only one monad in the sense of the *Phaedo*, this monad is not the actual subject of the mathematical reasoning; indeed Plato might not have noticed this, but it is corroborated by (3) above. Similarly the square as such is only one; but the reference to 'the square and the diagonal' (*Republic*, 511a) surely contains an allusion to the theorem that the square on the diagonal of a square is twice that square in area. This theorem mentions two squares. Again, Plato *might* not have noticed this; but one should not pile up too many discrepancies; and if he did think mathematicians grasped the forms, he contradicted himself flatly in the next book of the *Republic*.

Some have thought, and others have denied, that Plato introduced 'mathematicals' into the *Republic*. Mathematicals are not visible objects but not forms either; for there is only one form of the circle, let us say – but a mathematician has to speak of intersecting circles; yet the circles that he is speaking of are not the marks on a particular piece of paper or the indentations on a particular patch of sand; they are subjects of mathematical reasoning. Against the view that Plato introduced mathematicals it is objected that nothing like the foregoing point is made in the *Republic*; and Plato says that the mathematician's reasonings are "for the sake of the square as such and the diagonal as such". Nevertheless as we have seen he expressly speaks of several identical *ones* which mathematicians claim are in the numbers they are talking about. And in the passage about 'the square as such and the diagonal as such' (510d7) he speaks rather ambiguously: he does not actually say that these are what the mathematician is reasoning *about*, but only that the mathematician's reasonings are *for the sake* of these and that he is *trying* to see forms.

Since, however, he later reveals that the mathematician is trying to see what cannot be seen his way, but only by means of dialectic, what he actually grasps in thought is different. But it would in a way be wrong to say that Plato believed in the real existence of mathematicals. He only believed that mathematicians did. The mathematician "dreams of reality" but does not really get a vision of it (533b8). Since he *thinks*, he does good by drawing the soul away from preoccupation with the sensible world; but in relation to the true objects of knowledge his thinking, Plato says, is like the seeing of shadows and images in relation to the true objects of sense (534a5).

(5) So the philosopher who follows Socrates when asked to give an account of the hypothesis, namely that something is one, or two, or that there is a result 2 (2 comes about or something becomes two), will 'postulate another hypothesis' from among higher ones, whichever seems best, till he comes to 'something sufficient' (*Phaedo*, 101d5). It seems safe to equate this with the account in the *Republic*: he will make the hypotheses not into *principles* but really into hypotheses, i.e. stepping stones and jumping-off points, up to where he reaches what is unhypothetical, the principle of everything; he will lay hold of that, and fasten on to the things that are made fast by it, and so he will descend to the end, not using the sensibly perceived at all, but using forms themselves, through forms themselves, to reach forms themselves,

and so conclude with forms. The *Republic* reveals that this unhypothetical thing is the form of the good – thus claiming to sketch the fulfilment of Socrates' desire in the *Phaedo*.

Thus the postulated mathematical objects are themselves mere shadows and images of the forms – *they* do not get established by dialectic. They remain only the hypotheses of people who do mathematics and do not do dialectic. They are what mathematicians use drawings and other physical objects as images of (510d7) but are not the same as the forms the mathematician is pursuing his reasonings for the sake of. When the hypotheses are done away by dialectic proceeding from that sufficient unhypothetical first principle, and the philosopher advances from it in the establishment of real knowledge, he does not come to them. In knowledge, according to Plato, we have the unitary forms alone and through these discern that the mathematician in his reasonings was producing a mere conjectural picture of what we now possess.

But of course this only means that Plato disbelieved in mathematicals as Parmenides disbelieved in the various and changeable world. So no wonder we get the Academy developing mathematicals as Aristotle describes, although the pure form doctrine is the only theory of the really real, and a 'two worlds' dichotomy is constantly taught in the dialogues. The objects of mathematics and geometry which are not yet forms aren't obtrusive enough to qualify as a whole intermediary world. They are an unreal half-way house, intelligible shadows of the real seen on the upward path from things of sense to the forms, but it takes mathematical enquiry to reveal them. And naturally mathematicians remain in their half-way house, so it is intelligible that belief in the mathematicals should be ascribed to Plato. His attempt to derive numbers as forms in the *Parmenides* is a mere exercise, sketchy and unconvincing.

3　The New Theory of Forms

I want to suggest that Plato arrived at a revised theory of forms in the later dialogues. Or perhaps I might rather say that he constructed a new underpinning for the theory. This can be discerned, I believe, in the *Sophist*, taken together with certain parts of the dialectic of the *Parmenides* which use the same language as the *Sophist*.

Here is an analogy for the new theory: a laminated sheet divided into two halves which can be folded one upon the other so as to coincide in their exterior boundaries. The whole represents the totality of beings. Let us suppose this diptych to be lying open. The bottom layer corresponds to being, the next to unity, the next to identity. These laminations are common to both sides, which otherwise differ.

In the left half of the diptych patterns are stamped. Any pattern is stamped right through all three layers. The patterns correspond to the forms of the early theory – except, indeed, the form of the good. But patterns may divide into parts which are also patterns.

The right half of the diptych represents *the other*, or *being different from*. The bottom three laminations have no holes in them. But there are very many further leaves on this side, as many as there are distinct patterns stamped on the left side. Each such pattern has a leaf of the right side which corresponds to it by having its shape cut out there, so that the shape of the pattern is there a hole instead of a formation of the material, and so that this hole coincides like a mirror image in position and shape with the stamped pattern on the left side.

We now suppose the diptych shut. For every pattern the perpendicular geometrical projection through the whole thickness gives us the part of *being*, of *the one*, of *the same*, and the numberless parts of *the other*, that belong to it.

In offering this analogy I am treating as key themes:

(1) The study of *one, whole* and *part* in the later dialogues
(2) The conception of certain forms as 'parcelled out'
(3) The problem of negation.

Plato's writing touching the forms may be divided into the naive and the sophisticated or reflective. 'Naively' he says that e.g. good itself is one and simple and that the forms *are* being, or being is the forms. When he becomes sophisticated he reflects immediately on his own formulations; for example he applies his theory to what they introduce. Must not there be being itself? This question would perhaps have greatly startled and perplexed him when he wrote the *Phaedo*. "We say that *just* itself, and *beautiful*, and *good* is

From *The Monist* 50, 3 (1966).

something . . . I am talking about them all, about size for example, health, strength, and, to give all the rest in a single word, about their being – whatever each of them *is*." (65d) Forms were being; their general designation was "that which itself is" (75d); the *being* of a thing is named after the expression "what is" (92d).

Any thesis about *being* offered at that stage would be a blanket thesis about the forms. In the *Sophist* Plato reflects on *being* as something other than what is said to be, and in turn on *other* itself. Reflecting on the whole, on being, on one, on same and other, he formulates a theory of the intercommunion of certain forms. Being, same and other 'run through' all things; and, as I shall argue, he regards them all as having parts. This doctrine of *being, same* and *other* as 'running through' one another and everything else, is clearly the origin of the Aristotelian Scholastics' doctrine of 'transcendentals' which 'run across' all the categories. We can infer from *Parmenides*, 144, that *one* should be added to the list.

Greek itself worked with Plato to produce the early theory of forms. Few English words function grammatically so as to produce with a fair degree of naturalness the kind of effect that Plato can produce with most Greek terms. One that does is "fire". There are many fires, which get lit and put out; all these are fires because they have the characteristics of fire. It cannot be denied that fire itself is something, always the same. It is what fire *is*.

Fire, and substantial kinds generally (of which fire is one for an ancient), are not typical examples of Platonic forms. (See *Parmenides*, 130c.) The English reader must imagine that adjectives like "equal", "big", "just", could go naturally into sentences like the last four of the last paragraph. In Greek the form "the φ itself" – functioning like "fire itself" – is natural for every noun or adjective φ; Greek naturally forms "the many φ's" for any noun or adjective φ. Adjectival predicates of plural subjects go into the plural; they can also always form subjects without the aid of a word "thing(s)". In Greek a term functioning as a predicate is commonly without an article. And finally, the Greek for "what is", which may be followed by a predicate-expression, is equally Greek for "what exists".

Upon the whole I follow Geach[1] and Moravcsik[2] in preferring to avoid the abstract nouns sometimes used by Plato and far more often used by his translators to render his expressions for forms. The reason is that with such nouns, self-predication, which for Plato is a constant feature of forms, often seems too absurd.

When Plato speaks of 'good itself', or says that the beautiful itself exists or is something, we have not yet got the theory of forms. This is supposed to be a generally admissible starting-point. From it indeed, we pass over smoothly into formulations that are explicitly theoretical, embodying the "worthwhile hypothesis" of the *Phaedo* (92d). Of course, we might say, fire itself is

[1] 'The Third Man Again', *Studies in Plato's* Metaphysics, ed. R. E. Allen (London, 1965).
[2] 'Being and Meaning in the *Sophist*', *Acta Philosophica Fennica* Fasc *14*, (1962).

something. That fire is itself one thing, to which fires have an obscure relation, – to say this would be to set it up as a Platonic form.

The transition from "something" to "one thing" is easily made to seem compulsory by Greek. The alternative to "something" is "nothing" – in Greek, "not one" (*Parmenides*, 144b, 165e; *Sophist*, 237d–e). But even without benefit of this trick of Greek the transition 'not nothing – therefore something with a numerical identity which one has before one's mind' may seem inescapable (cf. Wittgenstein meeting the accusation that he makes a sensation into 'a nothing', at *Philosophical Investigations*, 304). So we have a slide from the innocuous-seeming "φ itself is something" to a doctrine of the separate existence of this unitary nature, φ-itself. φ-itself would be 'simple', in that it is *merely* what being φ *is*; and changeless in that being-φ is *being*, not becoming. Hence we get the full-blown doctrine of a whole world of these simple, unitary changeless natures. (This separateness, Aristotle's bugbear about the forms, is certainly indicated in the *Phaedo*. But I cannot find that the word for it is used until Plato has begun to write critically about the theory of forms.)

The doctrine of intercommunion of forms might not seem to belong especially to Plato's 'sophisticated' thought. Was this intercommunion not mentioned in the *Republic* (476c)? And that is a 'naive' passage: each of the forms is itself one, but appears many because of the communion of forms with bodies, with actions, and with one another.

The contrast is this: in the *Republic* the intercommunion of forms is being looked at only from the point of view of the form that is participated in by others, so as to appear many. In the *Sophist* the interest is rather in forms as participating in others.[3] It is as if Plato had caught himself saying that *the just itself* is and is one, and had realized that if 'the just itself' was what he wanted it to be in speaking of it – e.g. one – it was not the 'simple' form of the *Phaedo*. There he would have said that the just itself simply was the being expressed by "just" – but that is naiveté in using the word "being".

In the *Philebus* we find this sort of sophisticated reflection on calling the forms single. The passage (15a–b) is perforce obscure. It concerns the second of the three serious problems which, Socrates says, arise if we try to postulate one *man*, one *ox*, one *beautiful*, one *good*. "The first is whether we ought to accept some such monads as truly existent. Next how these – each of them being always the same and *not* susceptible of generation and corruption – nevertheless are unshakeably this *one*." The words "this *one*" are feminine and so must be understood to go with "monad". The thought is hard to discern. The argument seems to run somewhat as follows:

> The many men, oxen, beauties, and goods are subject to generation and corruption; this is one reason why they *are* not e.g. man, ox, the beautiful and the good (for these never change). Indeed they *are* not any of the things that are predicated of

---

[3] Mr Ackrill has adequately refuted Cornford's view that the intercommunion of the forms is symmetrical. See 'Plato and the Copula', in R. E. Allen, *Studies*.

them; hence no puzzle about the contrary things that may be predicated of them at different times, when the short grow tall, the light heavy, and so on. But those others existing imperishably would have to be this *one thing* that we called them. We called them single, each a monad. Perishing multitudes are not, any of them, any one thing; but how *are* imperishable monads just *that?*

What then is the puzzle about many forms' each being one? In *Republic* X, when arguing for there being only one of any form, Plato did not mention generation and corruption as proof that φ's were not *φ itself*; multiplicity was enough; as soon as we have several φ's, we know there is further the form, that one thing whose nature they have, which is *the* thing that *is* φ. So multiplicity of monads should be enough to prove that the forms *are* not *one itself*. Why then does Plato in the *Philebus* suggest there is a difficult problem about how they *are* monads? When he wrote the *Republic* he would presumably have thought simply that the form *one* appeared many by being participated in by bodies, actions, and other forms.

If however we turn our attention to the forms that do the participating (as opposed to the form that is participated in) we are struck by the fact that the unity of each is essential to its being characterizable as a form at all. In the *Republic* itself, when the demiurge was supposed to have made two pattern beds, it had to follow that another *one* appeared, which was the form that both shared in; and here, in the *Philebus*, we are discussing the postulation of *one* – *man, ox, beauty* or *good*. No wonder "much zeal for division turns into perplexity" (the literal rendering of 15a7 as the MSS have it); for if we divide the *one* from the *man, ox,* the *beautiful* and the *good*, ought we to say that those monads really exist; and how can they be monads?[4]

In the *Republic* Plato wrote as if the communion of forms in forms were the same as the communion of anything else in forms. The later dialogues suggest an eventual conviction that this could not be true.

As regards the *Sophist* it is fair to suppose that there must be a lot of connection between the Eleatic visitor's criticism of the Friends of Forms and his criticism of Parmenides; i.e. that Plato believed both theories, though superficially unlike, to be really based on the same mistake. This mistake, and hence the connection, is easy to discern: it is that of refusing to admit that φ-itself is ever also describable as not φ. Parmenides himself had thought this way about being, teaching that one must not include non-existents in what is, or say that what is, is not. Similarly about *same*: he is reproachful about saying that something is the same (as one thing) and not the same (as another). He had inferred that there can be no variety, multiplicity or change in being, which is wholly and thoroughly one.

[4] Editors have emended the text at several points without grounds in the MSS. because they could not follow the thought. The text shows that there are supposed to be three 'serious questions'. The first is whether these monads must be judged to exist, and the third is how they are related to the infinitude of becoming. Interpreters generally fail to distinguish the second problem from one of the two others. My interpretation sticks closely to the text, which it leaves intact, and discerns three quite distinct problems, the second of which it does indeed take philosophical acuteness to notice.

In the *Parmenides* Plato seizes on *one*, not on *being* for his exhibition of 'dialectic'. Parmenides had not been concerned with any such notion as that of *the one itself*, but with being; thus the connection with him seems at first sight rather associative and superficial, and one wonders why he is the man who is made to indicate that the forms will be all right if backed up by a proper dialectic.

The dialectic which follows doubtless shows, or is meant to show, much that I have no grasp of. But two things emerge. One, that it is hopeless to argue that whatever φ may be, being φ belongs only to φ itself among forms, and hence that ψ itself cannot be φ. We must not suppose that Plato had thought this the right way to argue before the *Parmenides*; the parts of the dialectic where this is assumed as a principle are an illuminating *Gedankenexperiment*. It is used, for example, in the first hypothesis (139c): *one* will not, *qua* one, be different from anything, because it does not belong to *one qua* one to be different from anything – this belongs *only* to the *different from another*. Thus *one* will not be different by being one, i.e. not by itself: hence *one* in itself will not be different. This is a conclusion we could more readily accept than the method of proof; there is even something right about it, in that nothing, *qua* single, is differentiated from anything else. But as a proposition about *one itself* it is insane and the argument for it is intolerable. The results of the first hypothesis are indeed explicitly granted to be generally unacceptable.

If we could not ascribe anything to any form except itself, we might straightway conclude that we could not say that φ *is* φ – for only being *is*. Thus we could hardly say anything about anything. We might rather maliciously truncate the argument by remarking that we can still say – and can only ever say – "Being is." Plato reaches the conclusion that we cannot say that *one* is or is one in a more roundabout way and does not point out this truly Parmenidean conclusion. But it is pretty obvious and is one more pointer to the genuine connection between Parmenidean thought and consideration of the theory of forms. For the dialectic of the *Parmenides* is a contribution to the question what can be said about a form.

To reject that insane principle is to accept the intercommunion or interweaving of forms, and according to Plato the possibility of propositions and reason depends upon this. Parmenides himself said much more than "being is" such as "all else is mere names", and it is easy to see he was thus naive: he is here wide open to the typical criticism of the sophisticated Plato. For if there are so much as names, there is something that isn't being itself. This could be shown by the sort of argument used against Parmenides in the *Sophist*, in relation to *one*. Is the name other than the one? If so, there is more than the one; but if the name is the same as the one, what must in that case be permissible substitutions in "the name is the name of the one" yield the nonsense "the one is the one of the name" (244d). The Parmenides of the dialogue produces a comparable, though less witty argument: *is* and *one* must differ, otherwise one could put "one one" for "one is". In comparison with the historical Parmenides this could be called sophisticated.

Thus Parmenides is preparing the way for the *Sophist*, not merely by showing the necessity of the interweaving of forms, but also by his considerations about *one, part* and *whole*. This is extremely important. Not merely is it of interest in itself, but Plato is going to use the concepts of part and whole to explain the intercommunion of forms.

At 142d–c and 144c Plato's Parmenides comes to apparently contradictory conclusions about the relations of one, part and whole. In the first passage the one being is a whole of parts, *one* and *being*; the one in it has being and the being is one, so each part in turn is after all not one but two, and so on *ad infinitum*. It is only the whole that is one; any part is only part of a whole.

In the second: if a part exists it must be one part. This unity of each of the parts, being simply a case of "one found at once in many places", will never make a whole. Since, then, the infinite plurality of numbers can be generated by considering one as being, and being is divided up into as many numbers as there are, one itself is infinitely divided, each of the numbers being one.

There are at least three antinomies in these passages taken jointly: the *one* that exists both is and is not a whole; parts both are and are not unit parts; parts both do and do not constitute a single whole. When considering parts that are parts of a whole, Plato's Parmenides cannot concede unity to them severally because they are infinitely subdivided; when considering an infinite set of parts of being, each single, he cannot concede wholeness to the set.

Combining the two sets of conclusions, he has the result that the *one* that *is* is one and many, whole and parts, bounded and infinite, but makes no attempt to reconcile these opinions by showing how "one" could apply at once to the parts collectively as parts of a whole, and to them severally when each was a distinct number. It looks as if "one" was supposed to apply only one way at a time.

Certain sketches of philosophy, and of Christian theology, have been bedevilled by a confusion about the question whether something was one. For example, "Is God one?" is ambiguous between "Is there only one God?" and "Has God internal unity?" We have been greatly helped, in sorting this matter out, by the work of Frege. Following him rather than Plato for the moment – though our purpose is to elucidate Plato – let us attach "one" and "many" to concept-words and speak of one φ and many φ's: one and many men, one and many squares, one and many positive integers. Note that, for this move to be useful, the predicate 'φ' has to be 'countable'; that is to say, it must be determinate what is one and what are two quite distinct φ's.

We may speak indifferently of the form, or of the class, presented by the open sentence "x is φ"; for present purposes, any difference between Plato's forms and the classes of modern set theory is immaterial. But the relation of whole and part, being transitive, is a quite different one from that of form and particular instance, or class and member. Thus if we speak of one φ among many φ's, since we should not speak of the class of φ's as a whole composed of φ's as parts, the many φ's do not in general compose a whole of any sort, let alone a whole φ. Frege objected to the question "How many?" or "How many things?" If asked "How many are there?" we need to know "How many *whats*?" and the answer must be a countable predicate "φ". We must observe that the question "How many parts?" is just as objectionable as "How many things?" unless it is clear in context how parts are meant to be counted.

If the noun after "one" or "many" is "part", we need to know 'part of what?' Here we should notice two possible styles of answer, differentiated by English (though not Greek) idiom. We may be told "of a φ" or "of φ": e.g. 6 pieces of an apple, or 6 bits of apple. Let us postulate an answer of the first kind, namely "of one φ" where "φ" is a countable predicate, and let us consider one φ divided into several parts; each, we can say, is one separated part – I suppose each to be quite separated off from the others. It is clear that the unity of the parts taken together, which is found in them because they are parts of one φ, is not a case of *one* being found 'simultaneously in several places', any more than of φ's being found simultaneously in many places. But the singleness of each single part is of course a case of *one* being found 'simultaneously in many places', and so is comparable to the singleness of each of the many φ's in relation to the property of being φ. Indeed, properly speaking it is an instance of that, because we have modified the term "part", in "separated part" in such a way as to turn it into just such a countable predicate φ: the question "How many separated parts has this dismembered watch?" is usually answerable without asking what is to count as a single separated part.

Plato is treating "one" rather as if it were such a predicate 'φ' and noting what results we get if we consider his 'one that is' as divided into parts. In the first argument, his principle of division does not in any way characterize the parts so as to give us a countable predicate; thus we may justify his saying that such a part is not one. The only *one* thing is the given whole of all these parts from which he started. In the second, he has a principle of generating no end of parts, all of which are single numbers; so each of these parts *is* one, but the unity in question yields no whole.

We come now to the discussion in the *Sophist* that touches on this theme. Characteristically, it starts from scratch, not assuming that any breach has been made in the plausible seeming principle: "The truly one must be without parts." The argument goes as follows:

> There is nothing against what has parts being subject to *one* as affecting all the parts, and thus being a totality and a whole and in this way one. But what is subject to *one* in this way cannot itself be *one itself*. If we reason right, we have to say that the truly one is without any parts at all. The question is, is being *affected* by *one*, so as to be one and a whole, or are we to deny totality of being? This is difficult, for: (1) if being somehow one is an affection of being, being is clearly not the same as *one* and all will be more than one. Whereas (2) if being at any rate is not affected by *one* so as to be a whole, but the whole itself does exist, then being will be less than what is;

and it will be deprived of itself and will not be being, and once more all becomes more than one, with *being* and *whole* each having assumed its own separate nature. But (3) if the whole has no existence at all, then the very same holds of being; and in addition to not being, it will not ever come to be either. For whatever comes to be comes to be as a whole (245a–d).

One's first thought in reading this passage is that it trades sophistically on the ambiguity between the question "Are beings wholes?" and "Is there such a thing as the whole of being?" But we are at the starting-post; the differences between the working of such a word as "being" and such a word as, say, "apple" have still to be characterized.

Further observations on the passage: "the whole itself" is a much preferable rendering to "wholeness". The question is not one as to whether a certain abstract property exists; otherwise there could be no inference from the non-existence of the whole to the non-existence of being at (3). We may say: Isn't this a frightful sophistry? Beings may well not form a totality; therefore the question whether 'the whole' exists may be answered "No" without implying that nothing exists. But that beings do not form a totality is itself a very obscure thought: one might say that the beings that there are must be all the beings that there are, so if there is not such a totality, there are not any. We should have to determine whether a totality, in the sense of *all*, is different from a whole: a question raised explicitly in the *Theaetetus*, and implicitly by Quine's treatment of mass terms as proper names of single scattered objects.[5]

The whole passage is concerned with Parmenides' one (i.e. sole) being and seems directed first at proving that there must be more than one being. But we must note that the issue of all the possibilities considered – and they are meant to be *all* the possibilities – is intolerably paradoxical. The only way for being to be a whole is for there to be more than this whole. Whereas, if being is not a whole, whether there is such a thing as the whole or not, being will not be.

We are not meant to be left with these results. These considerations show that we have got to construct some sort of account of how *one, being, part, whole*, and other forms presenting comparable difficulties are related among themselves and to other ones. It is much as if in modern philosophy one opened discussion with a set of propositions and reasonings about meaning which were evidently unacceptable, but whose unacceptability showed that our apparatus for handling the relevant questions needed to be amplified.

We have observed that the common feature of the early theory of forms and the philosophy of the historical Parmenides is the interdict on any sort of contradictory predication: whatever φ may be, φ-itself cannot be in any way describable by an opposite of φ. In that part of the *Parmenides* which deals with the forms we have Socrates saying that he would be utterly amazed if "like and unlike, one and many, rest and motion could combine . . ." (129e). But inthe dialectical exercises of the *Parmenides* the interdict yields

[5] *Word and Object* (Cambridge, Mass., 1966), p. 98.

such hopeless consequences that the ground is well prepared for abandoning it. In the *Sophist* we have to judge that the *same* is *different* from being, rest, motion and difference. So the principle is infringed for *same* and *different*; as, also, for *one* and *many* (if these can be called contraries). Nevertheless it is not wholly abandoned: it is five times insisted upon for *rest* and *motion*.

Further, the Eleatic visitor wishes to say that he does not infringe it in the case of being: not-being is not an opposite of being, as, we may suppose, black is of white, or large of small. Not to be is to participate in the *other* of being: not to be φ, to participate in that part of the other which stands over against φ.

I do not see that Plato distinguishes between 'the copula of predication' and identity by his theory that participation in a form φ is compatible with participation in the other of φ. That could be said already to be done (if one is very keen on such a formulation) by his familiar distinction between participating in φ and being φ *itself*. It is only in such more extreme, experimental, passages of dialectic as *Parmenides* 139c, that we have arguments suggesting that φ can be predicated *only* of φ itself. It is true that once we have the apparatus, motion's not being the same as such and such is explained as motion's participating in *the other* in respect of such and such. But the means of making the distinction have not been lacking: motion and rest cannot either of them be being, because being is ascribed to them and neither can be ascribed to the other.

No: what Plato is concerned with all the time is the possibility of contradictory predication: that something may be both φ and not φ (and that in particular sometimes φ itself may also be not φ). Thus motion is the same and not the same; the same by participation in *the same* with regard to itself, and not the same by participation in *the other* in regard to a host of forms. And so, indeed, for all forms. There is, he says, nothing to object to in this.

"Participation in the other of φ" is a formula used *not* merely for nonidentity with φ. This may escape one's attention because participation in the other of φ by a form is often non-identity with φ. But we must not forget that falsehood is to be explained as the mixture with *saying* of non-being (260b–c), and that non-being has previously been explained as the other of being (259a8). This admixture of 'the other of being' cannot consist in non-identity of the form *saying* with the form *being*. Rather, "the other of being" holds, i.e. is truly predicable, of what is said.

Theaetetus' flying is 'being which is other than being' (263b11), ascribed to Theaetetus by the false proposition "Theaetetus is flying" (263b). It is clear that we can also put: "Theaetetus is not flying" *i.e.* "Theaetetus is other than flying"; not meaning that he is doing something else, but that *the other of flying* holds of him. For Plato has told us that "not big" is not an expression for the small or equal and that "not beautiful" is the name of the *other of the beautiful*, which is precisely other than nothing but *the beautiful* (257). "Not flying" then, we may infer, is the name of the other of *flying*.

Thus "Theaetetus is not flying" is not to be identified with " 'Theaetetus is flying' is false". The former predicates of Theaetetus the other of flying, the latter predicates the other of being of what is said about Theaetetus in "Theaetetus is flying".

This makes what is said a bit of non-being, i.e. of the other of being, when "Theaetetus is flying" is said and is false. And, in one sense of "what is said" *this* makes what is said different according to whether it is true or false. Not, however, in any *prima facie* intolerable sense: we may rather compare Frege's doctrine that the false proposition is the name of a different object (the False) from what it would have been a name of if it had been true (whereas he rejects the intolerable supposition that sense depends on truth-value).

To refer to my diptych analogy, when we consider "Theaetetus is flying" we will look to the pattern of *flying* stamped on the left side. This will be a part of being to which Theaetetus is related by the (unexplained) relation of participation if the proposition is true. But if the proposition is false, no participation of Theaetetus in any form corresponds directly to its being false; the speaker has in fact (whether he knows it or not) named a bit of non-being. That is to say, he has as it were hit that part of the outermost layer on the right hand side of the diptych which would be marked out by a perpendicular projection from the 'flying' pattern. Thus the falsehood of the false proposition has a close correspondence with the truth of the negative one. The lines of projection from the pattern will pass on the right side through the boundary of the hole in that leaf which represents the *other* of the pattern.

If I am right, then the idea of some forms as having parts is of extreme importance. In the *Sophist* (258d–e) it is especially stressed that *the other* is divided up into many bits and parcelled out among all things in relation to one another, and we hear of the part of the other that stands over against the *being* of each, or, if we follow Simplicius, of each part of the other that stands over against being. I prefer the MSS reading, but on my interpretation it makes no difference to the sense. For the language of being divided up and parcelled out occurs also in the *Parmenides* in relation to *one* and to *being* (144), and it seems immensely unlikely that this part of the argument there was not also part of Plato's final view. This gives us three points: (1) the being and unity of each form are parts of being and of the one respectively; (2) the one being is a whole of parts, among which are the existent unitary forms of the early theory; (3) each existent form is a whole composed of the form and its being. Thus there will be a part of *the other* (the bottom right hand layer in my diptych as it lies open) which is a part of being that stands over against being. This part of the other will itself be divided into parts each of which stands over against part of being, i.e. the being *in* one of the forms of the early theory. We may add that *one* will, like being, same and other, "run through" everything, and *same*, like being, one and other, will be "parcelled out" among all things.

In connection with negation, the very advantages for which Plato embraces his theory pose a problem. Non-being is part of being; so to say something is not φ does not quite generally exclude its also being φ. Of course, this was just what Plato wanted: but now, if we have this, how do we ever get exclusion?

We may pause to take very brief stock of the problem of negation. If something's *not* being the case is nothing, then we wonder how we are saying something true by saying that something is not the case. Again, if James' absence is a nothing when James is absent, how is it distinguished from John's absence, when John is absent as well? On the other hand we must not think that "A is not red" is without more ado equivalent to "A is yellow, *or* blue . . . etc.", to understand "not *p*" we cannot run to what is or may be the case *instead* of *p*, and use this to explain why "not *p*" says something.

Suppose, then, we decide that there is something in the idea that "It is not beautiful" says "It is other than beautiful" or: the negative proposition uses the negated proposition to fix a possible being-the-case whose sole characteristic is to be *other* than what is said by the negated proposition. The question then arises: why should we then not have both *p* and not *p*?

If "not *p*" says *nothing* about the subject matter of "*p*", how does it *say* anything? If it says something, how can that exclude anything else?

We saw that Plato does not want automatic exclusion of φ by not-φ. But he does want it sometimes. Take rest and motion. Rest participates in the other with regard to motion. That, however, may simply mean that it is not the same as motion; it would leave it possible for rest to move, and this Plato does not want. We seem left with having to say "Rest does not participate in motion" in order to explain "Rest does not move". But then either this, or the language about being, is anomalous. "*x* does not exist" was not "*x* does not participate in being" but "*x* participates in *non*-being". At least in the case of being it must be granted that "*x* participates in the other of φ" does duty *both* for "*x* is not the same as φ" and "*x* is not φ". If we take "Rest participates in the other of motion", in the same two ways, i.e. as meaning either "Rest is different from motion" or "Rest participates in non-motion" we probably do not depart from Plato; if it is a fault not to distinguish these, he certainly commits it in regard to being, and does not make out that being is quite exceptional. But even if we have "Rest participates in non-motion" that is still compatible with "Rest participates in motion". Are we simply left with non-participation, refusal to combine, or the part of these forms? What is being *wholly other than* – Plato's expression for the relation of rest and motion (225e)?

Further: what about Theaetetus not flying? *That* will present us with a problem of how to exclude "Theaetetus is flying"? Why not both at once? Once more: if not flying is a sort of form, then how does it exclude any other?

It is possible that the peculiarities of participation by forms in being, one and same hold for all participation by forms in forms. That is to say, when a form A participates in a form B, this is by A's being as it were a pattern in a part of B. B, let us say, the more generic form, is a sort of grain stamped on to a part of one-being-same; and A a further pattern stamped into part of this grained area.

To adopt this suggestion would be to take up a hint from the first part of the *Parmenides*. Parmenides asks whether when the many φ's participate in a form, the relation in question is that of being covered by the form, one by one part of the form and another by another. For forms and particulars the suggestion seemed hopeless; for forms and forms it might be profitable. It certainly fits Plato's account of participation by forms in the transcendentals: and there seems to be no reason to think that he did not regard these as simply supremely generic, so that the same model ought to work for more ordinary genera in relation to their species (certainly Plato was much concerned with the proper division of kinds in all his later philosophy). Incompatibility – being wholly other than – will then be *not being a part of*. And, with the exception of the transcendentals themselves, negative forms will be incompatible with their positive correlates in the same sense.

It nevertheless remains obscure why this last sort of incompatibility should carry over to particulars; why Theaetetus cannot be flying and not flying. He can be at rest in one way and in motion in another. Thus incompatibility of forms with one another does not automatically carry over; so cannot Theaetetus be flying too, when he is not flying?

I leave the question as it stands because my purpose is only exegesis and so far as I know Plato offers us no solution. We know that Aristotle (*Metaphysics*, IV, iv) had an immense struggle, almost incomprehensible to us, to argue that being φ excluded being not φ and not being φ, and that one of the ideas he had to contend with was that being φ was compatible with not being φ because it was compatible with being ψ and being φ was not being ψ.

In spite of these difficulties raised by his theory, Plato does not want to canonize contradictory and opposite predications. It is easy to find superficial contradictions, he says, but this is childish, and it is no serious refutation of a man to detect them in what he says. The serious business is to follow a man's arguments and show that he has said that the same is different in the relevant way, and vice versa. That is: simply to show that the same is different and the different the same, the big small and the small big, and so on, is a foolish game anyone can play. And if a man is arguing, you don't refute him by showing he has treated the same as different, etc. But if he has taken two things as the same in some particular way, to show that they are different *in that way*, or that he has said they are: that is the serious refutation (259c–d). Thus Plato's aim is to restrict and clarify objectionable contradiction while retaining an unobjectionable kind, rather than be stuck with Parmenides or the early theory of forms.

The man who can do such refutation will be the dialectician. He is marked precisely by his 'adequate discernment' of the different sorts of one-many relation that we get when we consider different types of relations among forms:

Dialectical science makes divisions according to classes, and does not take the same kind to be different or a different kind to be the same. If you can do this, you will adequately discern (i) a single form wholly penetrating many things, each found single and separate, (ii) many forms, mutually different, comprised externally by a single form, (iii) a single form constituted by many wholes in one, (iv) many forms that are separate and wholly distinct. (*Sophist*, 253d)

This passage is obscure and of disputed interpretation. I believe it is usually taken that (i) gives the relation species – individual, (ii) genus – species, (iii) transcendentals – other forms, (iv) perfectly specific forms considered in themselves. This interpretation is indeed rather closer to the text than others; yet I think it does not weigh every word sufficiently, together with the arguments which we have considered as so important in the *Parmenides* and the *Sophist*.

I suggest:

(i) and (ii) make the contrast between a form φ such that if a lot of things are φ each is one single distinct φ, and such forms as 'one', 'whole', 'being', which do not function so, and are conceived to contain other forms in an external fashion. (See 250b where rest and motion are said to be comprised by being; and for other relevant verbal and doctrinal echoes, *Parmenides*, 142e, 145c.) Thus genera in relation to individuals belong to (i) no less than species do. (iii), on the other hand, appears to me to concern the genus–species division though more obscurely: possibly we get (iii) wherever one could find many wholes gathered together in some sort of unity, as: many species in a genus, or many elements in a complex, i.e. letters in a word or particular characteristics in a man (cf. *Theaetetus*, 209c). (iv) Finally, the many forms that are wholly separate and distinct apparently are so much so as not to provide any sort of one–many contrast like the other three. It appears to me that nothing discussed in the *Sophist* corresponds to this, but something which I have already mentioned from the *Parmenides* does: the series of natural numbers is there treated as a series of such forms.

4 Understanding Proofs

Meno, *85d9–86c2, Continued*

Purely by questioning Socrates has elicited from an uninstructed slave the conclusion that the square on the diagonal of a square is twice the original square in area. Then comes a part of the dialogue which I translate:

Socrates. This knowledge, then, that he has now, he either got some time, or always had?

Meno. Yes.

Soc. Well, if he always had it, he was always a knower. But if he got it at some time, he is not in a position of having got it in the present life. Or has someone taught him to do geometry? For he will do just the same for the whole of geometry and all the rest of mathematics. Is there anyone who has taught it all to him? You ought to know, especially as he was born and brought up in your household.

Men. I know that no one ever taught him.

Soc. But he has these opinions. Or hasn't he?

Men. He must have them, obviously, Socrates.

Soc. But if he did not get them in the present life, isn't it clear that in some other time he had them and had already learnt them?

Men. Obviously.

Soc. Well, isn't that the time when he was not a human being?

Men. Yes.

Soc. If, then, true opinions are to be in him during the time both that he was a human being and that he wasn't, and these opinions when elicited from him by questioning become knowledge, won't his soul have been learned for the whole of time? For it's clear that for the whole of time he either is or is not a human being.

Men. Obviously.

Soc. If then the truth about real things is always in our soul, the soul is immortal. So oughtn't you boldly to try to search out and be reminded of what you find you don't know now, which is what you don't remember?

Men. Somehow you seem to me to speak well, Socrates.

Soc. And to myself, Meno. For the rest, I shouldn't insist absolutely on the argument. But I should, if I could, absolutely do battle, both in argument and in action, for this: that if we think that we must search out what

From *Philosophy*, 54 (1979).

anyone is ignorant of we shall be better and braver and less lazy than if we think that it is impossible to find out what we don't know and that we need not search for it.

I continue the dialogue:

Men. I am sure I agree with what you have just said, Socrates. But when I think again of what I have already assented to, I feel a doubt. Though you would not insist on the argument, yet it is not a small matter whether what you said and I agreed to was right. Or is it?

Soc. No, far from small. So tell me your doubt.

Men. That the slave, before he was a human being, already had and had learnt these opinions seems to me to be proved beyond doubt. But why should you say his soul is therefore immortal? May he not have existed for a little time before he became a human being, and in that little time have acquired these true opinions?

Soc. Well, Meno, let it be as you say. But if he acquired these opinions at some time, either someone taught him them, or no one, but he somehow acquired them by himself. Do you agree?

Men. Yes.

Soc. Then if someone taught him, what kind of teaching do you imagine it to have been? To explain what I mean, did you not tell me that no one taught him geometry, and did I not learn this from you?

Men. Yes.

Soc. Then you taught me that?

Men. Yes.

Soc. And I understand it?

Men. Obviously you understand it, Socrates.

Soc. Do I just understand it, or do I also believe it to be true? Wait a moment, and you will see what I mean. Could I understand it and not believe it or believe it and not understand it, or must I do both if I do either?

Men. If you understand that no one taught him geometry, you also believe it.

Soc. But what if you were to be deceiving me, and someone did teach him? Should I be understanding nothing or something?

Men. I am in doubt about this, Socrates, because I have often heard that if you say what is false you say nothing, and so it seems that if you are deceived by me you have understood nothing. Yet in some way you have understood something, for you have understood what I said and I said no one taught him geometry. I don't know how this is something if it is not true, yet it seems to me I said something and you understood what I said even if you were deceived.

Soc. Shall we then refuse to be tempted by this question, how what is false is something, and say that nevertheless I understood something?

Men. Yes.

Soc. Is it not possible for me to have disbelieved you?

Men. Yes, indeed.

Soc. And should I not be disbelieving what I understood as much as, if I had believed you, I should be believing what I understood?

Men. Obviously.

Soc. Then when you tell me no one taught this slave geometry, I may understand you and not believe you? But is it possible that without understanding I should believe you?

Men. Surely not, Socrates, for what you believe you must first understand.

Soc. Who made me believe the slave had not learned geometry? You, or someone else?

Men. I did.

Soc. Then did you also make me understand what you made me believe? I mean, did you make me understand in such a way that I also could have disbelieved?

Men. No, for if I say I made you understand I make no difference between understanding and belief, but if I make a difference, then it was not I but someone else who made you understand what I was going to say.

Soc. Then let us return to the geometrical truth which, you say, he acquired a little time before he became a human being, and which we are both supposing someone taught him. Did this person teach him just as you taught me that he had never been taught geometry?

Men. I suppose so.

Soc. That is, by telling him?

Men. Yes.

Soc. But first he must have understood, must he not? For you said that one first understands and then believes.

Men. Yes. That is, he understood in such a way that he did not yet know whether it was true.

Soc. But when he was told it was true, and believed it, then he knew it was true? What divine authority told him, Meno, and why should he have to believe what he was told?

Men. I suppose he was not merely told but himself perceived that it was true.

Soc. Then it was not because he was told, but because he himself perceived that it was true, that he knew? But if so, why did he need a teacher? Or couldn't the teacher have done what I did and so done as well as by telling him or even better?

Men. Yes, that is clear.

Soc. Then if you suppose that he was taught, you will find that this teaching could be nothing but reminding. Or if he did not himself perceive that what was said was true, but nevertheless believed it and learned to say it as a result of being taught, would you then say he knew?

Men. No indeed, he cannot know such things unless he himself perceives that they are true, or get anywhere by only repeating what he has been told.

Soc. Not even if he is told proofs and told that they are proofs?

Men. No, not if he only repeats it.

Soc. But if he himself perceived that these opinions were true then these opinions were already in himself and he was only reminded.

Men. Yes.

Soc. Then he certainly knew these things or had true opinions of them before any teaching?

Men. Yes, certainly.

Soc. Well, let us try the second possibility that I mentioned.

Men. The second? What was that?

Soc. That he was not taught but that he just at some time acquired these opinions by himself.

Men. Yes, that must certainly be the case.

Soc. In what way do you think he acquired them? Or that they came to be in him so that afterwards whenever he was taught or questioned he was reminded of them, whether he was taught or questioned before he was a man or afterwards? But before we ask this I think we have got to go back on our tracks, because if I am not wrong we have made a mistake which will mislead us. I mean when we said: a man first has to understand what he afterwards believes, but when he understands he can deliberate with himself or someone else whether what he understands is true or false.

Men. Why, Socrates, how could there be a mistake about that?

Soc. As far as concerned what you told me, when you said no one taught the slave geometry, I do not know if there was a mistake, but if there is no mistake as far as concerns geometry, then we shall fall into unsurmountable difficulties, if I am not wrong.

Men. What difficulties?

Soc. Suppose that you were considering the proof of that same true opinion that I recalled to the mind of the slave, do you think that you could first understand the proof, not knowing whether it was true or false, and then find out somehow that it was true?

Men. Yes, that is what I think.

Soc. Then you find out, from something or by reason of something, that the proof is a true proof?

Men. Yes, I suppose so.

Soc. But will not what you find it out from, or the reason by which you find it out, be the proof that the proof is correct? Now do you see a part of the difficulties we have summoned up?

Men. Yes, I see them, since you will ask about this proof in turn whether it can be first understood and then seen to be correct. But why do you call this only a part of the difficulties?

Soc. Because I believe there are many more. In a proof one says "therefore" and "if . . . then . . .", and such things, does one not?

Men. Yes.

Soc. And what does one understand in understanding these words?

Men. That the truth of what is finally said follows from what is first said.

Soc. Does one understand that it follows, or that it is said that it follows?

Men. Why, both.

Soc. Then one understands that it follows?

Men. Yes, since one understands both that it follows and that it is said that it follows.

Soc. But if it follows and in understanding what is said with "therefore" or "if . . . then . . ." one understands that it follows, then one knows, and all the more believes, that it follows, as soon as one understands what is said and not later.

Men. That cannot be right, Socrates, since false proofs are given of many things and one finds out that they are false. If what we said was right a false proof would be nothing. I want to deny what I said before, and say that one understands only that it is said that it follows.

Soc. But does one understand what is said?

Men. Yes, certainly.

Soc. Namely, that it follows.

Men. But we agreed, Socrates, not to be tempted by this problem of the false, and your argument now is just the one that we avoided about the false statement that the slave had not learned geometry. One understands this expression, "it follows", but in such a sense that understanding does not mean believing.

Soc. I believe we cannot avoid that problem here, Meno, whether or no we were right before. But that we were then not altogether wrong is something I think I can show, in a way that may persuade you that we nevertheless cannot avoid the question here. For in the case of the slave, when I understood you even without believing you, did I understand what you said?

Men. Of course you did.

Soc. And could I or could I not learn afterwards that what you said was true, even though I now regard it as doubtful?

Soc. If it were true you could.

Soc. But if I afterwards learn that something does follow, when before I regarded it as doubtful whether it followed, doesn't that show that I was wrong before?

Men. Yes.

Soc. But in the case of the slave, was I wrong to think it doubtful?

Men. Yes, if it was in fact true.

Soc. Then I ought always to believe what is in fact true, even without reason?

Men. Yes, by my present argument.

Soc. But don't consider just your present argument, but what is really the case. Is there such a thing as an irrational true opinion, as when a jury is convinced by false rhetoric that something is the case, and it is in fact the case, but not for the reasons for which they have believed it?

Men. Yes.

Soc. Then someone who remained in doubt in such a case would be less deceived than the others?

Men. Yes.

Soc. But someone who thought it doubtful whether something followed that did perfectly follow would be wrong, and would pass from error to truth when he saw that it followed, while someone who was doubtful about the guilt of a criminal who was guilty would not be wrong, and would pass, not from error, but from ignorance to truth when he saw that the criminal was guilty, real proofs turning up.

But what does one understand to be said, Meno, when one understands "therefore", or that it is said that it follows?

Men. Let me say for the moment, that one understands that this case is like what really does follow, and like precisely in following.

Soc. Then in what really does follow, does one first understand and then believe that it follows?

Men. Really I do not know what to say about that.

Soc. Will you not say with me that where one perceives following one does not first understand what is said in "This follows from that" and then perceive that it is true, though it might have been false without this making any difference to what one understood in understanding it? As for the cases where there is a doubt, the doubt comes of not understanding, not from the doubtfulness of that which is understood. Though you understand "since" and "if then" and "therefore" and "follows from" and though you understand me if I say that I am shorter than you, and also if I say that your slave is handsome, still you will not understand me if I say that since I am shorter than you your slave is handsome; and either you will never understand because there is nothing to be understood, or when you understand at that same moment you will know the truth of what I say, and not at separate moments. So what you thought absurd is in fact true and a false proof is nothing though it pretends to be something. But I spoke of many difficulties in saying that in proof and mathematics we do not first understand and then believe, and I have mentioned only a few. There is one other that I will mention.

Men. Wait, Socrates, if you do not mind.

Soc. No, why should I mind?

Men. What you have just been arguing concerns proof, not the truths of geometry and the rest of mathematics. While I may agree that I cannot understand a proof and yet not know that it is correct, nothing you have said obliges me to say the same about mathematical truths. Why do you throw them into your remarks as if you had proved something about them?

Soc. I have heard it said, Meno, that mathematical truths are the same in this regard as proofs, and that you do not understand them if you do not see that they are true. You yourself have agreed that you cannot know them from being told them. If you could understand them without knowing them, couldn't you know them simply from being told them by those who do know? For everything that results from knowing depends on understanding, but can be known to be true if only you have information that what is understood is true; but once that information is given, understanding is enough. In that case, why should it matter how the information is given, so long as it is given somehow? But if understanding and knowledge are ever the same, then it will not be possible simply to be told, and, whether it is proof or mathematics or some other subject matter as well that we have not touched on at all – whatever cannot be known by one who is merely told it and learns to repeat it will be such that understanding and knowledge are the same and error is impossible: but what poses as saying something and would commonly be called error is saying nothing.

Men. Well, what were you going on with when I interrupted you?

Soc. A further difficulty about first understanding and then acknowledging, which does bring in mathematics and does not only refer to proof. When I persuaded your slave to recall what he already knew, and he said that the square on the diagonal was equal to twice the original square, about what was he showing that he had true opinions?

Men. About squares and areas.

Soc. Which ones? Was it for example about these figures that I drew on the ground?

Men. No, certainly not, for I noticed you drew them rather carelessly and what was said was not true of them.

Soc. Would we have known it was true of them if I had drawn them with the greatest possible care? Or should we have needed to have recourse to something else to find that out?

Men. What else?

Soc. To measurement.

Men. Yes, that is what we should have had to do.

Soc. Then the squares and areas about which the slave recalled his true opinion were not these nor any he could observe either in this life or in any other, if by observing you mean perceiving by means of the senses.

Men. This is quite familiar to me, Socrates. But why should he not, a little before he became a human being, have seen with the eye of his soul the real squares and areas that are the objects of geometry?

Soc. Wait, Meno, you are hurrying the argument on too fast. We are still thinking whether understanding and knowing are the same or different, and if I am not mistaken, answering this question will help us with the other. Do you imagine that when the soul's eye looks at intelligible objects such as the objects of mathematics, what it sees is related to it as colour is to the natural eye or rather as are body and shape and everything else besides colour that we learn to distinguish using our faculty of sight?

Men. Could you explain more clearly the distinction that you are making?

Soc. I will try, but I do not know if I shall succeed. What I have heard is that colour and sight are connatural. If anyone sees at all, he sees colour, and there is nothing else that he necessarily sees, not even figure or size. But colour and sight are twins, generated together and inseparable. Hence if sight could judge and say what it saw, what it would have to say if left uninstructed would be nothing but the name of the colour that it saw for the moment. In this alone it would need no instruction and it would mean this by whatever it uttered, without any danger of error, for it would mean the colour that it saw and its understanding what it meant and knowledge that what it meant was present to it would be the same thing. But anything else it needs instruction to judge and it learns to judge rightly, and is also able to judge wrongly and therefore understanding and knowledge are distinct. What I am asking you is whether when the soul views intelligible objects it views them as the eye views colour, or judges them as sight judges other things?

Men. I have no idea what to say.

Soc. Try and see if you won't find something to say. Did I not say that sight needs instruction to judge anything but colour?

Men. You did.

Soc. But if one is instructed one is instructed by someone, isn't one?

Men. Yes.

Soc. But did we not agree that the soul cannot be instructed by anyone in its knowledges, because whatever instruction it can at any time be given will only be reminder?

Men. Yes.

Soc. Do you not say, then, that the soul views all intelligible objects, when it views them, as the eye views colour, and does not judge about them getting instruction how what it says should be made to correspond to what it sees? Therefore it is not able to judge rightly or wrongly about what it sees, understanding what it says without knowing it to be true and afterwards finding out and acknowledging that it is true.

Men. Yes, it seems that I say all that.

Soc. But when the soul has forgotten what it once knew, then, when it is reminded of it fragmentarily and with difficulty, its true opinions, which have been quiescent in it all the time, are awakened and it knows them in understanding them and could never be told them or made to understand them without knowing them.

Men. Forgive me, Socrates, if I am willing to doubt what I have been most sure of. But why should we not say that in what is called learning, the soul is not reminded of what it once saw, but now for the first time opens its eye to the objects about which it is taught? I was convinced that what is called learning is not really learning but recollection by the arguments we have gone through, namely that without being told a man discovers the truth, and, as we now have seen, that he could never be told either in this life or at any other time but must perceive the truth of himself if he is to know it; and further because those things about which he discovers the truth are not the things before his bodily eyes which the teacher points to, such as diagrams. Since, then, these are all he has before him, but by the help of them he is led to say what is true about other things, and can see how these objects here fall short of those other things, I agreed that he was reminded of them. But now it has struck me that perhaps he has the real things before his mind's eye, and the diagrams serve not as reminders but as signposts. The reason why these truths cannot be taught is that a teacher can only draw his attention to signposts and hints whereby he opens his intellectual eye and looks in the right direction and now utters and sees the truth of what he says about the real mathematical objects that he is looking at. If it should be possible to say this, then it makes an end of all the argument about the immortality of the soul.

Soc. Well argued, Meno. But you will not object if we scrutinize your argument to see if we should keep it or reject it?

Men. Certainly I shan't mind.

Soc. Didn't you agree just now that when the soul saw the real, this could be compared with sight when it sees colour and not with sight when it learns to judge what an object is, as: a horse, or a man, or of what size or at what distance it is?

Men. Yes.

Soc. Now answer this, if you can: does sight work to see colour? I mean, must it labour and be trained and have practice and will it stumble and make mistakes, producing utterances which mean nothing though it supposes them to mean the colour that it sees? Or did we agree that if left only to announce the colour that it saw, it would be without error, for there is no place for error or instruction but what it utters means what it sees, and its understanding of what it means and its knowledge that what it means is present to it are identical?

Men. I think I see what you mean, and that I must say that sight does not have to do any hard work in order to see colour.

Soc. But doesn't a pupil have to do a great deal of hard work in order to master geometry, and still more to learn dialectics, and doesn't he need much training and practice and make what are commonly called mistakes while he is learning, and still sometimes also when he is advanced? (Though you and I have agreed that these so-called mistakes are utterances in which he somehow fails to say anything though he seems to be saying something.)

Men. Yes, that is true.

Soc. Then, Meno, he cannot have the forms and mathematical objects present to his soul's view when he has to work and makes mistakes, but he stumbles and gropes like a person trying to remember, and what he does manage to remember he remembers piecemeal and using many aids and a great deal of hard work.

Men. Yes, Socrates, I only needed to be reminded in order to return to my former conviction that what is called teaching is really reminding. But can you show me how all this argument about knowing and understanding helps the main purpose of our discussion? It still seems to me that we have proved only that the soul must have existed for some time before this life, and not that it always existed.

Soc. Did we not say that sight and the object of sight were twins, generated together?

Men. Yes.

Soc. And is there not a kinship between twins?

Men. Obviously.

Soc. Then are not the soul and what it understands similarly twins? and so kin?

Men. No, it is the soul's understanding and its objects that are twins, as it is sight and colour, not the eye and colour, that are twins.

Soc. Very well. But now tell me this: do the objects of the soul's understanding come into existence? I mean, in the cases that we are talking about. For that it comes about that the slave is taught or not taught in this life, is something that comes into existence. But do the square and the diagonal and their relations come into existence?

Men. No.

Soc. Then if the soul's understanding and these objects are twins, neither did the soul's understanding ever come into existence.

5   Aristotle and the Sea Battle

De Interpretatione, Chapter IX

(1)   For what is and for what has come about, then, it is necessary that affirmation, or negation, should be true or false; and for universals universally quantified it is always necessary that one should be true, the other false; and for
singulars too, as has been said; while for universals not universally quantified it
is not necessary. These have been discussed.

For what is and for what has come about: he has in fact not mentioned these,
except to say that a verb or a tense – sc. other than the present, which he
regards as the verb *par excellence* – must be part of any proposition.

it is necessary: given an *antiphasis* about the present or past, the affirmative proposition must be true or false; and similarly for the negative. An *antiphasis* is a
pair of propositions in which the same predicate is in one affirmed, in the
other denied, of the same subject. Note that Aristotle has not the idea of the
negation of a proposition, with the negation sign outside the whole proposition; that was (I believe) invented by the Stoics. – What Aristotle says in
this sentence is ambiguous; that this is deliberate can be seen by the contrast
with the next sentence. The ambiguity is first sustained, and then resolved at
the end of the chapter.

for universals universally quantified: he does not mean, as this place by itself
would suggest, that of "All men are white" and "No men are white" one
must be true and the other false. But that if you take "All men are white" and
"No men are white" and construct the antiphasis of which each is a side,
namely, "All men are white – Not all men are white" and "No men are white
– Some man is white", then one side of each antiphasis must be true, and the
other side must be false.

for singulars too, as has been said: sc. of "Socrates is white – Socrates is not
white" one side is necessarily true, the other necessarily false. (This is what a
modern reader cannot take in; but see the 'Elucidation'.)

for universals not universally quantified: his example rendered literally is "man is
white – man is not white". From his remarks I infer that these would be correctly rendered "men are . . .". For, he says, men are beautiful, and they are
also not beautiful, for they are ugly too, and if they are ugly they are not

beautiful. I believe that we (nowadays) are not interested in these unquantified propositions.

These have been discussed: i.e. in the immediately preceding chapters, by which my explanations can be verified.

(2) But for what is singular and future it isn't like this. For if every affirmation and negation is true or false, then it is also necessary for everything to be the case or not be the case. So if one man says something will be, and another says not, clearly it is necessary for one of them to be speaking truly, if every affirma-
(3) tion and negation is true or false. For both will not hold at once on such conditions. For if it is true to say that something is white or is not white, its being white or not white is necessary, and if it is white, or not white, it is true to say or deny it. And if it is not the case, then it is false, and if it is false, it is not the case; so that it is necessary as regards either the affirmation or the negation that it is true or false.

singular and future: sc. there will be a relevant discussion tonight; this experiment will result in the mixture's turning green; you will be sent down before the end of term.

it isn't like this: namely, that these propositions (or their negations) must be true or false. Throughout this paragraph the ambiguity is carefully preserved and concealed.

it is also necessary for everything to be the case or not be the case: the Greek "or" is, like the English, ambiguous between being exclusive and being non-exclusive. Here it is exclusive, as will appear; hence the "or" in the conditional "if every affirmation and negation is true or false" is also exclusive, and to point this he says "every affirmation and negation", not, as in (1) "every affirmation or negation"; that "or" was non-exclusive.

For both will not hold on such conditions: namely, on the conditions that every affirmation is true or false. This condition is not a universal one; it does not apply to the unquantified propositions, though if the "or" is non-exclusive it does. But if the conditions hold, then just one of the two speakers must be speaking the truth.

It is true to say or deny it: ἦν is the common philosophical imperfect.

(4) So nothing is or comes about by chance or 'whichever happens'. Nor will it be or not be, but everything of necessity and not 'whichever happens'. For either someone saying something or someone denying it will be right. For it would either be happening or not happening accordingly. For whichever happens is not more thus or not thus than it is going to be.

'whichever happens': the Greek phrase suggests both "as it may be" and "as it turns out". "As the case may be" would have been a good translation if it could have stood as a subject of a sentence. The 'scare-quotes' are mine; Aristotle is not overtly discussing the *expression* "whichever happens".

is not more thus or not thus than it is going to be: as the Greek for "or" and for
"than" are the same, it is so far as I know a matter of understanding the
argument whether you translate as here, or (as is more usual) e.g.: "isn't or
(sc. and) isn't going to be rather thus than not thus". But this does not make
good sense. Aristotle is arguing: "We say 'whichever happens' or 'as the case
may be' about the present as well as about the future; but you don't think the
present indeterminate, so why say the future is?" Or rather (as he is not
talking about the expression): "Whatever happens will be just as deter-
minately thus or not thus as it is."

> (5)   Further, if something is white now, it was true earlier to say it was going to be
>   white, so that it was always true to say of any of the things that have come
>   about: "it is, or will be". But if it was always true to say: "it is, or will be", then:
>   impossible for that not to be or be going to be. But if it is impossible for some-
>   thing not to come about, then it is unable not to come about. But if something
> (6)   is unable not to come about it is necessary for it to come about. Therefore it
>   is necessary that everything that is going to be should come about. So
>   nothing will be 'whichever happens' or by chance. For if by chance, then not by
>   necessity.

But if it is impossible for something not to come about, then it is unable not to come about:
the reader who works through to the end and understands the solution will
examine the dialectic to see where it should be challenged. It will turn out
that the point is here, in spite of the equivalence of the two Greek
expressions. The dialectic is very powerful; in spite of having familiarized
myself with the artfulness of the chapter, I cannot read this passage without
being momentarily convinced.

> (7)   Still, it is not open to us, either, to say that neither is true, as: that it neither
>   will be nor will not be. For firstly, the affirmation being false the negation will
>   not be true, and this being false the affirmation won't be true. – And besides, if
>   it is true to say that something is big and white, both must hold. And if they are
>   going to hold tomorrow, they must hold tomorrow. And if something is
>   neither going to be nor not going to be tomorrow, 'whichever happens' won't
>   be. Take a sea-battle, for example: it would have to be the case that a sea-battle
>   neither came about nor didn't come about tomorrow.

Still, it is not open to us, either, to say that neither is true: and yet Aristotle is often
supposed to have adopted this as the solution.

For firstly: this goes against what he has shown at the end of (3): "if it is false, it
does not hold". So much, however, is obvious, and so this is not a very
strong objection if we are willing to try whether neither is true. What follows
is conclusive.

And if they are going to hold tomorrow: from here to the end of the paragraph the
argument is: if it is the case that something will be, then it will be the case that
it is. In more detail: you say, or deny, two things about the future. If what

you say is true, then when the time comes you must be able to say those two things in the present or past tenses.

'whichever happens' won't be: i.e. 'whichever happens' *won't* happen.

(8)   These are the queer things about it. And there is more of the sort, if it is necessary that for every affirmation and negation, whether for universals universally quantified or for singulars, one of the opposites should be true and one false, that there is no 'whichever happens' about what comes about, but that everything is and comes about of necessity. So that there would be no need to deliberate or take trouble, e.g.: "if we do this, this will happen, if not, not".

(9)   For there is nothing to prevent its being said by one man and denied by another ten thousand years ahead that this will happen, so that whichever of the two was then true to say will of necessity happen. And indeed it makes no difference either if people have said the opposite things or not; for clearly this is how things are, even if there isn't one man saying something and another denying it; nor is it its having been asserted or denied that makes it going to

(10) be or not, nor its having been ten thousand years ahead or at any time you like. So if in the whole of time it held that the one was the truth, then it was necessary that this came about, and for everything that has been it always held, so that it came about by necessity. For if anyone has truly said that something will be, then it can't not happen. And it was always true to say of what comes about: it will be.

These are the queer things about it. And: I have diverged from the usual punctuation, which leads to the rendering: "These and similar strange things result, if . . .". This seems illogical.

e.g.: often rendered "since": "since if we do this, this will happen, if not, not". This does not appear to me to make good sense. The Oxford translator sits on the fence here.

So if in the whole of time it held: one must beware of supposing that Aristotle thinks the conclusion stated in the apodosis of this sentence follows from the condition. It only follows if the previous arguments are sound. He is going to reject the conclusion, but there is no reason to think that he rejects the condition: on the contrary. The last two sentences of the paragraph are incontestable.

(11) Now if this is impossible! For we see that things that are going to be take their start from deliberating and from acting, and equally that there is in general a possibility of being and not being in things that are not always actual. In them, both are open, both being and not being, and also both becoming

(12) and not becoming. And plenty of things are obviously like this; for example, this coat is capable of getting cut up, and it won't get cut up but will wear out first. And equally it is capable of not getting cut up, for its getting worn out first

(13) would not have occurred if it had not been capable of not getting cut up. So this applies too to all other processes that are spoken of in terms of this kind of possibility. So it is clear that not everything is or comes about of necessity, but

with some things 'whichever happens', and the affirmation is not true rather than the negation; and with other things one is true rather and for the most part, but still it is open for either to happen, and the other not.

take their start: literally: "there is a starting point of things that are going to be". The word also means "principle". A human being is a prime mover (in the engineer's sense), but one that works by deliberating. As if a calculating machine not merely worked, but was, in part, precisely *qua* calculating, a prime mover. But Aristotle's approach is not that of someone enquiring into human nature, but into causes of events and observing that among them is this one.

acting: he means human action, which is defined in terms of deliberation; see *Nichomachean Ethics*, VI, 1139: there he repeats the word "ἀρχή": "ἡ τοιαυτη ἀρχη ἀνθρωπος": *the* cause of this sort is man. An animal too, or a plant, is a prime mover. Hence his thought is not that there are *new* starting-points constantly coming into existence; that would not matter. It is first of all the nature of deliberation that makes him think that the fact of human action proves the dialectic must be wrong. I cannot pursue this here; though I should like to enter a warning against the idea (which may present itself): "the nature of deliberation presupposes freedom of the will as a condition." That is not an Aristotelian idea.

things that are not always actual: things that are always actual are the sun, moon, planets and stars. Aristotle thought that what these do is necessary. The general possibility that he speaks of is of course a condition required if deliberation and 'action' are to be possible. If what the typewriter is going to do is necessary, I cannot do anything else with the typewriter. Not that this is Aristotle's ground for speaking of the general possibility.

in terms of this kind of possibility: I take it that we have here the starting-point for the development of Aristotle's notion of potentiality. The sentence confirms my view of the point where he would say the dialectic went wrong.

with other things one is true rather and for the most part: as we should say: more probable.

(14)   The existence of what is when it is, and the non-existence of what isn't when it isn't, is necessary. But still, for everything that is to be is not necessary, nor for everything that isn't not to be. For it isn't the same: for everything that is to be of necessity when it is, and: for it simply to be of necessity. And the same for what isn't. And the same reasoning applies to the antiphasis. For it is necessary that everything should be or not, and should be going to be or not. But it is not

(15)   the case, separately speaking, that either of the sides is necessary. I mean, e.g., that it is necessary that there will be a sea-battle tomorrow or not, but that it is not necessary that there should be a sea-battle tomorrow, nor that it should not happen. But for it to come about or not is necessary. So that since propositions are true as the facts go, it is clear that where things are such as to allow of 'whichever happens' and of opposites, this must hold for the antiphasis too.

The existence of what is when it is . . . is necessary: i.e. it cannot be otherwise. A modern gloss, which Aristotle could not object to, and without which it is not possible for a modern person to understand his argument, is: and cannot be shown to be otherwise. It will by now have become very clear to a reader that the implications of "necessary" in this passage are not what he is used to. But see the 'Elucidation'.

simply to be of necessity: there is a temptation to recognize what we are used to under the title "logical necessity" in this phrase. Wrongly, though: Aristotle thought that the heavenly bodies and their movements were necessary in this sense. On the other hand, he seems to have ascribed something like logical necessity to them; nor is the idea as undiscussable as it seems at first sight.

But it is not the case, separately speaking, that either of the sides is necessary: the ambiguity of the opening "it is necessary that an affirmation (or negation) should be true or false" is here resolved. And we learn that when Aristotle said that, he meant that if p is a statement about the present or the past, then either p is necessary or not-p is necessary. But this means that in order to ascribe necessity to certain propositions (the ones, namely, that are not 'simply' necessary) we have to be informed about particular facts. So, one may ask, what has this necessity got to do with logic? – Aristotle, however, states no facts, past, present, or future. (I do in what follows; I hope this will not prove misleading: the purpose is only didactic.) His results could perhaps be summarized as follows; we use indices $_p$ and $_f$ to the propositional sign to indicate present and past time references on the one hand, and future time reference on the other. Then for all p, p vel not-p is necessary (this covers the unquantified propositions too) and p_p is necessary vel not-p_p is necessary; but it is not the case that for all p, p_f is necessary vel not -p_f is necessary.

> This is how it is for what is not always existent or not always non-existent.
> (16) For such things it is necessary that a side of the antiphasis should be true or false, but not this one or that one, but whichever happens; and that one should be true rather than the other; but that does not mean that it is true, or false. So it is clear that it is not necessary for every affirmation and negation that this one of the opposites should be true and that one false; for it does not hold for what does not exist but is capable of being or not being; but it is as we have said.

whichever happens: sc.: it is a matter of whichever happens.

that one should be true rather than the other: cf. 'rather and for the most part' above; note that this is governed by 'it is necessary'; I infer that Aristotle thought that correct statements of probability were true propositions.

but that does not mean: ἤδη, logical, not temporal;[1] ἤδη works rather like the German "schon" (only here of course it would be "noch nicht"). ἤδη in a non-temporal sense is, like οὐκέτι, frequent in Greek literature. English translators of philosophical texts usually either neglect to translate it or mis-

[1] I am indebted to Miss M. Hartley of Somerville College for pointing this out to me.

translate it. For examples, see *Theaetetus*, 201e4; *Physics*, 187a36; *De Inter-pretatione*, 16a8, *Metaphysics*, 1006a16. Bonitz gives some more examples.

AN ELUCIDATION OF THE FOREGOING FROM A MODERN POINT OF VIEW

A. The Vice Chancellor will either be run over next week or not. And therefore either he will be run over next week or he will not. Please understand that I was *not* repeating myself!

B. I think I understand what you were trying to do; but I am afraid you were repeating yourself and, what is more, you cannot fail to do so.

A. Can't fail to do so? Well, listen to this: The Vice Chancellor *is* going to be run over next week . . .

B. Then I am going to the police as soon as I can.

A. You will only be making a fool of yourself. It's not true.

B. Then why did you say it?

A. I was merely trying to make a point: namely, that I have succeeded in saying something true about the future.

B. What have you said about the future that is true?

A. I don't know: but this I do know, that I have said something true; and I know that it was either when I told you the Vice Chancellor would be run over, or on the other hand when I said he wouldn't.

B. I am sorry, but that is no more than to say that either he will or he won't be run over. Have you given me any information about the future? Don't tell me you have, with one of these two remarks, for that is to tell me nothing, just because the two remarks together cover all the possibilities. If what you tell me is an Either/Or and it embraces all possibilities, you tell me nothing.

A. Can an Either/Or be true except by the truth of *one* of its components? I seem to remember Quine speaking of Aristotle's 'fantasy', that "It is true that either *p* or *q*" is not a sufficient condition for "Either it is true that *p* or it is true that *q*". Now I will put it like this: Aristotle seems to think that the truth of a truth-functional expression is independent of the truth values of the component propositions.

B. But that is a howler! The 'truth' of Either *p* or not *p* is determined, as you know very well, by its truth value's being T for all possible combinations of the truth *possibilities* of its components; that is why its 'truth' gives no information. Having set out the full truth-table and discovered that for all possibilities you get T in the final column, you need make no enquiry to affirm the truth of $p \vee \sim p$ – any enquiry would be comic. If on the other hand you tell me $p \vee \sim q$ (*q* being different from *p*) you do give me some information, for certain truth-combinations are excluded. There is therefore the possibility of enquiring whether your information is correct. And that I do by discovering which of the truth-possibilities is fulfilled; and if one of the combinations of truth-possibilities which is a truth-condition for $pv \sim q$ is fulfilled, then I discover that your information is correct. But to tell me "It will rain, or it won't", is not to tell me of any truth-possibility that it is – or, if you like, will be – satisfied. Now will you actually tell me something about the future?

A. Very well. Either you are sitting in that chair or it will not rain tomorrow.

B. I agree, that is true, because I am sitting in this chair. But still I have been told nothing about the future, because since I know I am sitting in this chair I know what I have been told is true whether it rains tomorrow or not – i.e. for all truth possibilities of "It will rain tomorrow". But do you mind repeating your information?

A. Either you are sitting in that chair or it will not rain tomorrow.

B. (*Having stood up.*) I am glad to be told it will be fine – but is it certain? Do you get it from the meteorologists? I have heard that they are sometimes wrong.

A. But surely we are talking about truth, not certainty or knowledge.

B. Yes, and I am asking whether your information – which I agree is information this time – is true.

A. I can't tell you till some time tomorrow; perhaps not till midnight. But whatever I tell you then will have been so now – I mean if I tell you then 'True', that means not just that it will be true then but that it was true now.

B. But I thought it was the great point against Aristotle that 'is true' was timeless.

A. Yes – well, what I mean is that if I tell you – as I shall be able to – 'True' tomorrow – I mean *if* I am able to, of course – why, then it will have been, I mean is now correct to say it is true.

B. I understand you. If it is going to rain tomorrow it is true that it is going to rain tomorrow. I should be enormously surprised if Aristotle were to deny this.

A. But Aristotle says it isn't true that it is going to rain tomorrow!

B. I did not read a single prediction in what Aristotle said. He only implied that it didn't have to be true that it will rain tomorrow, i.e. it doesn't have to rain tomorrow.

A. What? Even if it is going to rain tomorrow?

B. Oh, of course, if it is going to rain tomorrow, then it necessarily will rain tomorrow: $(p \supset p)$ is necessary. But is it going to?

A. I told you, I can't say, not for certain. But *why* does that matter?

B. Can't you say anything for certain about tomorrow?

A. I am going to Blackwell's tomorrow.

B. And that is certain?

A. Yes, I am absolutely determined to go. (Partly because of this argument: it is a point of honour with me to go, now.)

B. Good. I fully believe you. At least, I believe you as fully as I can. But do I – or you – know you will go? Can nothing stop you?

A. Of course lots of things can stop me – anything from a change of mind to death or some other catastrophe.

B. Then you aren't necessarily going to Blackwell's?

A. Of course not.

B. Are you necessarily here now?

A. I don't understand you.

B. Could it turn out that this proposition that you, NN., are in All Souls today, 7 May 1954, is untrue? Or is this certain?

A. No, it is quite certain – My reason for saying so is that if you cared to suggest any test, which could turn out one way or the other, I can't see any reason to trust the test if, situated as I am, I have any doubt that I am here. I don't mean I can't imagine doubting it; but I can't imagine anything that would make it doubtful.

B. Then what is true about the present and the past is *necessarily* true?

A. Haven't you passed from certainty to truth?

B. Do you mean to tell me that something can be certain without being true? – And isn't what is true about the present and the past quite necessary?

A. What does 'necessary' mean here, since it obviously doesn't mean that these are what we call necessary propositions?

B. I mean that nothing whatever could make what is certain untrue. Not: if it is true, it is necessary, but: since it is certainly true it is necessary. Now if you can show me that anything about the future is so certain that nothing could falsify it, then (perhaps) I shall agree that it is necessarily true that that thing will happen.

A. Well: the sun will rise tomorrow.

B. That is so certain that nothing could falsify it?

A. Yes.

B. Not even: the sun's not rising tomorrow?

A. But this is absurd! When I say it is certain I am here, am I saying it wouldn't falsify it for me not to be here? But I am here, and the sun will rise tomorrow.

B. Well, let me try again: Could anything that can happen make it untrue that you are here? If not, I go on to ask: Could anything that can happen make it untrue that the sun rises tomorrow?

A. No.

B. If we continued in darkness, the appearance of the night being continued for the rest of our lives, all the same the sun will have risen; and so on?

A. But that can't happen.

B. Is that as certain as that you are here now?

A. I won't say. – But what does Aristotle mean when he says that one part of the antiphasis in necessarily true (or false) when it is the present or the past that was in question? Right at the beginning, when I said "The Vice Chancellor will either be run over or not, therefore either he will be run over or he will not" you said that I was repeating myself and could not fail to be repeating myself. And then you referred to the truth-table-tautology account of that proposition. But does not precisely the same point apply to what Aristotle says about "Either p or not p" when p is a proposition about the present or the past?

B. You could have avoided repeating yourself if you had said "The Vice Chancellor will either be run over or not, therefore either it is necessary that he should be run over or it is necessary that he should not be run over". But as you would have been disinclined to say that – seeing no possible meaning for an ascription of necessity except what we are used to call 'logical' necessity – you could not avoid repeating yourself.

Aristotle's point (as we should put it) is that "Either p or not p" is always necessary; this necessity we are familiar with. But – and this is from our point of view the right way to put it, for this is a novelty to us – that when p describes a present or past situation, then either p is necessarily true, or $\sim p$ is necessarily true; and here "necessarily true" has a sense which is unfamiliar to us. In this sense I say it is necessarily true that there was not – or necessarily false that there was – a big civil war raging in England from 1850 to 1870; necessarily true that there is a University in Oxford; and so on. But "necessarily true" is not simply the same as "true"; for while it may be true that there will be rain tomorrow, it is not necessarily true. As everyone would say: there may be or may not. We also say this about things which we don't know about the past and the present. The question presents itself to us then in this form: does "may" express mere ignorance on our part in both cases?

Suppose I say to someone: "In ten years' time you will have a son; and when he is ten years old he will be killed by a tyrant." Clearly this is something that may be true and may not. But equally clearly there is no way of finding out. (Unless indeed you say that waiting and seeing is finding out; but it is not finding out that it will happen, only that it does happen).

Now if I really said this to someone, she would either be awestruck or think me dotty; and she would be quite right. For such a prediction is a prophecy. Now suppose that what I say comes true. The whole set of circumstances – the prophecy together with its fulfilment – is a miracle; and one's theoretical attitude (if one has one at all) to the supposition of such an occurrence ought to be exactly the same as one's theoretical attitude to the supposition that one knew of someone's rising from the dead and so on.

As Newman remarks, a miracle ought not to be a silly trivial kind of thing – e.g. if my spoon gets up one day and dances a jig on my plate, divides into several pieces and then joins up again, it qualifies ill as a miracle, though it qualifies perfectly well for philosophical discussion of physically impossible but imaginable occurrences. Similarly if one were discussing impossible predictions one would take such an example as the following: every day I receive a letter from someone giving an accurate account of my actions and experiences from the time of posting to the time I received the letter. And whatever I do (I do random, absurd actions for example, to see if he will still have written a true account) the letter records it. Now, since we are dealing in what can be imagined and therefore can be supposed to happen, we must settle whether this would be knowledge of the future and whether its certainty would be a proof that what I did I did necessarily.

It is interesting to note that Wittgenstein agrees with Aristotle about this problem, in the *Tractatus*. "The freedom of the will consists in the fact that future actions cannot be known. The connection of knowing and the known is that of logical necessity. 'A knows that p' is senseless, if p is a tautology." We are therefore presented with the logical necessariness of what is known's being true, together with the logical non-necessity of the kind of things that are known. The 'logical necessity' of which he speaks in the remark on knowledge is thus not just truth-table necessariness. It is the unfamiliar necessariness of which Aristotle also speaks. "A knows that p" makes sense for any p that describes a fact about the past or present; so it comes out in Wittgenstein, and in Aristotle: past and present facts are necessary. (In more detail, by the *Tractatus* account: if A knows p, for some $q(q \supset p)$ is a tautology, and q expresses a fact that A is 'acquainted' with.)

Then this letter about my actions would not have been knowledge even if what it said was always right. However often and invariably it was verified, it would still not be certain, because the facts could go against it.

But could the facts go against the sun's predicted rising? Is there not a radical disagreement between Wittgenstein and Aristotle here: Aristotle thinks that it is necessity that the sun will rise, Wittgenstein says that we do not know that the sun will rise; and that the events of the future cannot be inferred logically from those of the present. But he also says that we could not say of a world not going according to law how it would look. So though he thinks that anything describable can happen, he would enquire whether the sun's not rising tomorrow is a describable event. So why does he say we do not know that the sun will rise? Not, I think, because the facts may falsify the prediction, but because there may not be any more facts: as in death the world does not change, but stops.

HISTORICAL TAILPIECE

The *De Interpretatione* was much read in the Middle Ages. In 1474 the following propositions on the truth of future contingents, put forward by Peter de Rivo, a university lecturer at Louvain, were condemned in a bull of Sixtus IV.

(1) In Luke, 1, when Elizabeth speaks to the Blessed Virgin Mary saying: "Blessed are you who have believed, because the things that have been said to you by the Lord will be effected in you", she seems to suggest that those

propositions, namely: "You will bear a son and call him Jesus; he will be great" etc., did not yet have truth.

(2) Christ, in saying after his resurrection: "It is necessary that all the things that are written about me in the Law of Moses and the Prophets and the Psalms should be fulfilled", seems to have suggested that such propositions were devoid of truth.

(3) When the Apostle says in Hebrews 10: "The law having the shadow of good things to come, not the very image of the things themselves", he seems to suggest that such propositions of the Old Law as were about the future did not yet have determinate truth.

(4) It is not enough for the truth of a proposition about the future that the thing will happen, but it is required that it should be inevitably going to happen.

(5) One of two things has to be said: either that there is not present any actual truth in the articles of faith about the future, or that the things they mean could not be prevented by the power of God.

These were condemned as 'scandalous and devious from the path of Catholic truth' and the said Peter withdrew them.

Thus the misunderstanding dates back at least to the fifteenth century.

Appendix

A Note on Diodorus Cronus

The question is, how the three propositions:

(i) What is true and past is necessary
(ii) The impossible doesn't follow from the possible
(iii) What neither is true, nor will be, is possible

are supposed to be incompatible.

The key to this must be found by considering how to use the unexceptionable (ii). Let us take something false, but possible if (iii) is right; then assume its truth and see what follows.

Take something of a kind to happen only once if it happens at all. Someone losing his virginity will do. Now let *the case* be that a given person neither is nor ever will be a non-virgin. However, it is apparently possible for him to lose his virginity. So we frame the proposition that he will. Does something impossible follow if this proposition is true?

It does follow that it will be true that he has lost it. But from the statement of *the case* this proposition, that he has lost it, will always be false and so, by (i), impossible.

There is a concealed assumption, namely:

If it always will be impossible that something has happened, then it always is impossible that it will happen.

This principle is highly specious, plausible. It may easily be assumed that something impossible at every point of time is simply impossible. But it is a false assumption. And it is not an impossibility *tout court* but only a future impossibility that can be derived from the proposition which is contrary to the case.

6   The Principle of Individuation

(1) I wish to express grateful admiration for the extreme clarity with which Professor Łukasiewicz has written.

He follows Aristotle in first taking:

Matter = material or stuff (e.g. bronze)
form = shape,

but his example of the same shape in different matter is a statue of bronze and a statue of stone. For Aristotle two bronze statues would also, and in just the same sense, be the same shape in different matter, and Professor Łukasiewicz's example is misleading because it naturally suggests that in calling bronze matter Aristotle is saying: "At this stage think of 'matter' as if it meant 'kind of stuff'." Aristotle says "This . . . individual, Callias or Socrates, is like *this* bronze ball, while 'man' and 'animal' are like 'bronze ball' in general",[1] and soon after comes the passage that Professor Łukasiewicz quotes: "The whole thing, such-and-such a form in this flesh and these bones, is Callias or Socrates; and they are different owing to their matter (for this is different), but the same in form (for the form is indivisible)." These passages show that two bronze balls would be a suitable example of the same shape in different material. Of course, both the concept of 'material' suggested by Professor Łukasiewicz's example, and the concept Aristotle is here concerned with, are familiar ones; both occur in Aristotle.

(2) *The absurdity of the idea of matter.* The hypothesis that things contain something which isn't anything and has no properties is certainly a senseless one, which, as Professor Łukasiewicz says, could not serve to explain anything. A book on logic by a philosopher Joseph, who used to be well known, expounds an argument that there must be an ultimate subject of predication which itself has no predicates. This parallels the Neo-Scholastics! The idea that what changes must be something that doesn't change precisely because it is what changes, is very like the idea that what has predicates must be something without predicates just because it is what has the predicates: both being based on inadequate reading of Aristotle.

(3) I am always uncertain what it means to call a concept "metaphysical".

---

[1] *Metaphysics*, Z, 1033b24: τὸ δὲ ἅπαν τόδε Καλλίας ἢ Σωκράτης ἐστὶν ὥσπερ ἡ σφαῖρα ἡ χαλκῆ ἡδί, ὁ δ' ἄνθρωπος καὶ τὸ ζῷον ὥσπερ σφαῖρα χαλκῆ ὅλως.

From *Proceedings of the Aristotelian Society*, supplementary volume 27 (1953).
Jan Łukasiewicz's contribution to the symposium precedes G. E. M. Anscombe's in the same volume.

But the concept of matter which Aristotle works on is at least an everyday one. If you show me a lump of stuff and tell me that it can be moulded into various shapes, that if you heat it it will turn into a gas, and if you electrify it it will turn into something else, I understand very well what you mean. Let me suppose that you show me a bottle of wine; you heat it, and it expands; you leave it, and after a while it has turned into vinegar. Now someone asks "But what is it *all* the time?" Some Greek philosophers would have wanted to say it was water or air or fire or something in between. "[They think that] there *must* be some nature, whether one or more than one, out of which the rest come to be while it remains constant."[2] Aristotle however wants to say: "There isn't anything which it is all the time. It *was* wine, and *is* vinegar, and there isn't some third thing that it is all the time." He says in the *Physics*, in the course of arguing against such philosophers: "Water and air aren't, and don't come, out of one another in the same way as bricks out of a house and a house out of bricks."[3] (One gets the point of this only by assuming with him that water and air [mist?] do in fact turn into one another.)

(It may be that we have a theory of chemical elements, so that if – to make the case simple – we identify something as a pure sample of an element, we go on saying that it is that element whatever happens to it. But any such theory – whatever its validity – is beside the point in our discussion, for it is necessarily based on the possibility of identifying the same bit of matter in our initial experiments: on our having the idea of 'nothing added and nothing taken away'.)

(4) We can see now why this matter (e.g. the stuff I have got in this bottle) is not as such a given kind of stuff (*τί*): for the same stuff was wine and is vinegar. Nor can we say that it is as such *not* a certain kind of stuff – for that would mean that it could not be, e.g., wine, and of course, when it is wine, it *is* wine. Similarly there are not any properties, either qualities or dimensions, which you can say it has – or lacks – *qua* this bit of matter. For example, if you told me that the process of change from wine to vinegar involved expansion or contraction, I should understand you, just as I understand the information I have about the expansion and contraction of water at different temperatures. So not even the volume determines the bit of water that we are talking about. This is what I understand Aristotle to be referring to when he says that matter is not as such (*καθ' αὐτήν*) so much (*ποσόν*).[4] Not that matter is: not even extended! – but that I cannot define the stuff (the bit of water, e.g., that I am talking about) as, e.g., "a pint hereabouts". It will perhaps be more than a pint if I cool it or less if I heat it. And the point about negation is clear here too: I cannot say that this stuff is as such *not* a pint; for perhaps it is

---

[2] *Met.* A, 983b17: δᾶει γὰρ εἶναί τινα φύσιν ἢ μίανἦ πλείους μιᾶς ἐξ ὧν γίγνεται τἆλλα σωζομένης ἐκείνης.

[3] *Physics*, I, iv, 188a15: οὐχ ὁ αὐτὸς τρόπος ὡς πλίνθοι ἐξ οἰκίας καὶ οἰκία ἐκ πλίνθων, οὕτω δε καὶ ὕδωρ καὶ ἀὴρ ἐξ ἀλλήλων καὶ εἰσὶ καὶ γίνονται.

[4] To be precise: not characterized by a particular answer to the question "How much?"

a pint, or I can make it a pint without addition or subtraction of matter.

That last word was being used in a completely familiar sense; and it is what Aristotle means by "ὕλη". (Only he tries to use it by analogy in all sorts of contexts, to extend its application away from where it is so to speak indigenous. I do not know or understand enough to have a general opinion whether the concept, in these extended applications, is so useful an instrument as Aristotle clearly thought it was. Certainly I feel only impatient when he considers calling units the matter of numbers. Nor, for instance, can I make anything of such an idea as 'place-matter'.)

I have approached Aristotle's idea of matter by way of '*this* matter'. He himself approaches it, in the first book of the *Physics*, in the context of discussions which are not alive for us and of most of which it would not be possible to give more than an external account. '*This* matter' is, however, Aristotelian. – Aristotle says that matter cannot very well be substance (οὐσία), because what specially belongs to substance is being separate and being a 'this something' (τόδε τι)[5]: e.g. 'this man', 'this cabbage'. Now 'this matter' is τόδε, but not τὶ: that is, it is designatable, identifiable, but is not as such of any specific kind or necessarily possessed of this or that property or dimensions, as I have explained. And it is of course not separable: that is, you could not entertain producing a specimen of it, which contrived to be of no kind (to be not τὶ). It is important to understand that this is a *conceptual* statement. That is, if I tell you that the stuff in this apparatus has changed from being water to being hydrogen and oxygen, you will show yourself quite at sea about the sense I am using the word "stuff" in, if you ask me to show you the stuff as it really is in itself, apart from being the various things it can be.

(5) I feel doubtful about Professor Łukasiewicz's comments on "matter in itself". For "matter in itself" does not seem to be used as a name or description by Aristotle, as I gather that "Ding an sich" may have been by Kant. You have to take the whole sentence in which "ὕλη καθ᾽ αὑτήν" occurs. Professor Łukasiewicz's comments strike me a little as if I were to say "A chair as such isn't upholstered or not upholstered", and were to be laughed at, not for the pedantic style, but for inventing such a strange object as 'a chair as such', with such extraordinary properties, whereby it defeated the law of excluded middle.

(6) Thus I do not think it reasonable to take exception to such statements as that matter is in itself indefinite and unknowable: it "has to be understood in what changes".[6] The change in question is substantial change: "For the rest (of the predicates) are predicated of the substance, while *it* is predicated of the matter."[7] That is, we say that milk, e.g., is white and liquid, and this

---

[5] *Met.* Z, 1029a26–30.

[6] *Met.* α, 994b26: τὴν ὕλην ἐν κινουμένῳ νοεῖν ἀνάγκη.

[7] *Met.* Z, 1029a22: τὰ μὲν γὰρ ἄλλα τῆς οὐσίας κατηγορεῖται, αὕτη δὲ τῆς ὕλης.

stuff is milk. But this stuff may be changed from milk into junket; nor apart from such changes should we have any such concept as 'this stuff', *as opposed to* 'this milk'.

> In all changes between opposed characteristics the subject of change is something: e.g. with change of place it is what is now here now there, with change of size what is now so much, now bigger or smaller, with change of quality what is now healthy, now sickly. Similarly with substantial change it is what is now in process of generation, now in process of destruction, now the subject as a 'this something' and now the subject in the way of privation.[8]

The last phrase is obscure. In order to explain what I think Aristotle means by it, I will consider a passage in Professor Łukasiewicz's paper. "It seems to be evident that all these things (bronze statues, stone balls, etc.) are individuals owing to their matter, as every bit of matter has at any time its own proper place and is different from all the other material things in the world." This leaves it open whether a given bit of matter, which at a given time has its own proper place and is different from all the other material things in the world, must be supposed always to have had, and always to be going to have, its own proper place and distinctness. If, that is, a given bit of matter is mixed and fused with, or absorbed by, another mass of matter, must we *a priori* suppose it to consist of particles retaining their identity? Aristotle's view of matter is a rejection and criticism of any such belief. Matter only has identity in so far as it is designate, earmarked; in itself it is indefinite (ἀόριστος). Suppose I throw a cupful of milk into the sea. It is no longer this milk; and if I ask where and what the stuff that I threw into the sea is, there is no need for there to be an answer beyond that it became part of the sea. And if in such cases there is an answer, this is because the particles continue to be identified by some property. For, if they are not marked out by anything, we cannot mark them out: if we do, they *are* marked out. And yet no one wishes to say that the stuff itself has been destroyed. We know no application for the idea of annihilation: by which I mean, not that we do not know of any case of it, but that we have – even side by side with a strong feeling of meaning for the word – hardly the vaguest notion what we should call a case of it. (Perhaps the total disappearance of a solid object, without a ripple in the surroundings except the inrush of air to take its place.)

Matter only exists as *somehow* designate; but that is not enough to secure the permanent identifiability of a once designate bit of it. And '*this* matter' is matter *thus* designate. (The usual criteria for speaking of the same stuff.) But when this matter loses its identity we do not speak of its being destroyed; and we say that *it* has lost its identity. This is what I take Aristotle to mean when he

[8] *Met.* H, 1042a33: ἐν πάσαις γὰρ ταῖς ἀντικειμέναις μεταβολαῖς ἐστί τι τὸ ὑποκείμενον ταῖς μεταβολαῖς, οἷον κατὰ τόπον τὸ νῦν μὲν ἐνταῦθα, πάλιν δ' ἄλλοθι, καὶ κατ' αὔξησιν ὃ νῦν μὲν τηλικόνδε, πάλιν δ' ἔλαττον ἢ μεῖζον, καὶ κατ' ἀλλοίωσιν ὃ νῦν μὲν ὑγιές, πάλιν δὲ κάμνον. ὁμοίως δὲ καὶ κατ' οὐσίαν ὃ νῦν μὲν ἐν γενέσει, πάλιν δ' ἐν φθορᾷ, καὶ νῦν μὲν ὑποκείμενον ὡς τόδε τι πάλιν δ' ὑποκείμενον ὡς κατὰ στέρησιν.

calls matter "now the subject as a 'this something', now the subject in the way of privation".

It is always, and especially here, important to notice that Aristotle's 'matter' is not a *hypothesis*.

(7) One may easily be puzzled by the expression "this matter, taken universally", which occurs for example in one of the passages quoted by Professor Łukasiewicz. What could be the point of, say, "this spot of light, taken universally"? The "this" seems to war with the "universally".

"This matter" contrasts with "undesignate matter", not with a general notion under which it falls as an instance. Hence when Aristotle wishes to generalize it, he says "this matter, taken universally".

(8) *On the analogy between bronze and its shape, and matter and form.* Aristotle's prime examples of 'substance' are: a man (ὁ τις ἄνθρωπος),[9] a horse, or, I might add, a cabbage. There is a contrast between a concept like 'cabbage' and a concept like 'gold'. Cabbage is not just a kind of stuff, but a cabbage is a particular thing; whereas the concept 'gold' does not determine an individual thing in this way. Had Aristotle written in English he would certainly have seized on certain peculiarities of English to make his point: we do speak of bronzes, marbles, irons, steels, woods (in bowls e.g.), glasses, etc. Bronze is to *a* bronze as flesh and bones etc. are to a man.

(9) "In a way, matter is obvious."[10]

(10) "Matter is in a way obvious, but . . . [form] is frightfully difficult."[11] Ross, for whom matter is most difficult, thinks that it is a concept reached by mentally stripping away all forms until you get to a characterless substrate. Aristotle regarded it rather the other way round: "by form I mean substance without matter":[12] that is, you get at it if you succeed in thinking matter away from substance. And he fell into frightful difficulties here, because he thought that form was the 'what' of substances: but of course the names of sensible substances and their definitions (e.g. "man", "two-footed animal") carry a reference to matter in their sense.

I do not understand Aristotle's 'form', and I do not yet know whether he got clear about it himself. Luckily I need not present my half-formed ideas about it here. (I wish Greek grammarians could determine something about the expressions "τὸ τί ἦν εἶναι", "τὸ τί ἦν εἶναι A", "τὸ εἶναι A", "τὸ A εἶναι" [A being a *dative!*], with which the *Metaphysics* is strewn. These queer constructions have escaped their notice.)

[9] *Categories*, 2a, 13.

[10] *Met.* Z, 1029a32: φανερὰ δέ πως καὶ ἡ ὕλη.

[11] *Met.* Z, 1029a32: φανερὰ δέ πως καὶ ἡ ὕλη· περὶ δὲ τῆς τρίτης [sc. τῆς μορφῆς] σκεπτέον, αὕτη γὰρ ἀπορωτάτη.

[12] *Met.* Z, 1032b15: λέγω δὲ οὐσίαν ἄνευ ὕλης τὸ τί ἦν εἶναι – cfr. supra 1032b2: εἶδος δὲ λέγω τὸ τί ἦν εἶναι ἑκάστου καὶ τὴν πρώτην οὐσίαν.

The difficulties that Aristotle gets into come out most clearly if we consider the following:

(1) A thing and its τὸ τί ἦν εἶναι are the same[13] (Anti-Platonic).

(2) τὸ τί ἦν εἶναι ἀνθρώπῳ and τὸ ἀνθρώπῳ εἶναι are clearly equivalent expressions.[13]

(3) ἄνθρωπος and ἀνθρώπῳ εἶναι are *not* the same unless you make ἄνθρωπος=ψυχή; which is right in one way, wrong in another.[14] It is clearly something special about 'soul' and 'circle' that they are the *same* as ψυχῇ εἶναι and κύκλῳ εἶναι.[15]

All this is supposed to be resolved[16] by the consideration that the form and the matter are the same, but one δυνάμει (in potentiality) and the other ἐνεργείᾳ (in actualization). But this is still Greek to me.

To translate "τὸ τί ἦν εἶναι": "the essence" produces gibberish – e.g. "Callias is of himself Callias and the essence of Callias."[17] It is clear that the correct gloss on τὸ τί ἦν εἶναι Καλλίᾳ in this passage is "man": "Callias is of himself Callias and a man". i.e. Callias is of himself that, to be which *is* being for Callias. Proper names do not, as some philosophers have said, 'have denotation but no connotation'; the criterion of identity for Callias is the criterion for there being the *same man* as the man we called "Callias".

I have mentioned so much about form, only because I want to consider the "grave inconsistency" which Professor Łukasiewicz ascribes to Aristotle. The inconsistency was this: Aristotle says that individuals are indefinable, but he also says that they consist of matter and form and that whatever has form has a definition. I do not think that Aristotle is in fact at all inconsistent at this point. The individual – say Callias– is indefinable, in the sense that there is no definition of him as opposed to another individual of the same species; his definition is the definition of the form. "Of the concrete substance in one sense there is an explanation (λόγος), in another not. For together with the matter there is none (for it is indefinite), but there is one according to first substance: e.g. the explanation (λόγος) of man is that of the soul."[18] But this passage and its context are thick with the difficulty that I have described, of which I do not understand the resolution. Hence the defence against Professor Łukasiewicz's particular charge is not worth much.

(11) I have the impression that Professor Łukasiewicz equates "this matter,

---

[13] *Met.* Z, 1031a17: ἕκαστόν τε γὰρ οὐκ ἄλλο δοκεῖ εἶναι τῆς ἑαυτοῦ οὐσίας, καὶ τὸ τί ἦν εἶναι λέγεται εἶναι ἡ ἑκάστου οὐσία. ἐπὶ μὲν δὴ τῶν λεγομένων κατὰ συμβεβηκὸς δόξειεν ἂν ἕτερον εἶναι, οἷον λευκὸς ἄνθρωπος ἕτερον καὶ τὸ λευκῷ ἀνθρώπῳ εἶναι.

[14] *Met.* H, 1043b2: ψυχὴ μὲν γὰρ καὶ ψυχῇ εἶναι ταὐτόν, ἀνθρώπῳ δὲ καὶ ἄνθρωπος οὐ ταὐτόν, εἰ μὴ καὶ ἡ ψυχὴ ἄνθρωπος λεχθήσεται· οὕτω δὲ τινὶ μὲν τινὶ δ' οὔ.

[15] *Met.* Z, 1036a1: τὸ γὰρ κύκλῳ εἶναι καὶ κύκλος καὶ ψυχῇ εἶναι καὶ ψυχὴ ταὐτό.

[16] *Met.* H *ad fin.*

[17] *Met.* Δ, 1022a26: ὁ Καλλίας καθ' αὐτὸν Καλλίας καὶ τὸ τί ἦν εἶναι Καλλίᾳ.

[18] *Met.* Z, 1037a26: ταύτης δέ γ' [sc. τῆς συνόλου οὐσίας] ἔστι πως λόγος καὶ οὐκ ἔστιν· μετὰ μὲν γὰρ τῆς ὅλης οὐκ ἔστιν (ἀόριστον γάρ), κατὰ τὴν πρώτην δ' οὐσίαν ἔστιν, οἷον ἀνθρώπου ὁ τῆς ψυχῆς λόγος.

taken universally", and "intelligible matter". This seems to be a mistake. "Intelligible matter" has to do merely with mathematical objects: on the analogy of sensible matter Aristotle invents 'intelligible matter' to account for the plurality of geometers' circles (e.g.). For when a geometer speaks of two intersecting circles he is not talking about, say, wooden rings. 'Intelligible matter' is an absurd and useless device, of no importance for Aristotle's account of material substance; and it is not 'intelligible matter' but 'this matter taken universally' that is said, together with the definition, to form universals like 'man' and 'horse'.

(12) Luckily it is possible to understand what is meant by calling matter the principle of individuation, without understanding about form.

It is not off-hand clear that there has to be a principle of individuation. If X and Y are different, the difference may be made clear by appropriate elucidation of the meaning of "X" and "Y".

Consider:

(1) "X and Y are numbers." – "Which numbers?"
(2) "X and Y are men." – "Which men?"

Both might be answered by giving a 'definite description'. For example "the even prime"; "the smallest integer, greater than one, that is both a square and a cube"; "the philosopher who drank hemlock"; "the philosopher who wrote the *Republic*". Before we accept the definite description we have to be satisfied that it applies, and in only one case. But, for (1), what satisfies us shows that a man will be contradicting himself, or talking nonsense, if he says "But still there might be another . . .". For (2) this is not so.

But isn't there pointing? – if, at least, the man is there to be pointed to? Pointing doesn't discriminate: you must know *what* you are pointing at. If I point, and say "That is X", and point again saying "That is Y", nothing in this situation shows that X and Y are not the same. It is of no use to say "But suppose I point to something different?" – for that is just what is in question: what is something different?

It is also of no use to appeal to definition by means of place and time; for this you require points of origin, and for points of origin you have to mention actual objects and events: individuals. No individual is pre-eminent. If I define an individual X by describing its spatial and temporal relation to another individual Y, and Y has no definition, then my definition of X is infected by the lack of definition of Y.

An individual can be defined by pointing and saying what (e.g. a man) you are pointing at. But this means that there is no difference between the definition of two individuals of the same species. You cannot say it lies in the difference between two acts of pointing, for nothing prevents one from pointing twice at the same thing; and you cannot say: but the difference is that you were pointing at *different* things; the different is not first merely a different *thing*, and then, in virtue of this, a different X.

Thus there is no definition of individuals except the definition of their kind. What, then, is the difference between two individuals of the same kind? It is difference of matter; and if I am asked to explain that, all I can do is, e.g., to cut something up and show you the bits. That is what is called material difference. This is what is meant by calling matter the principle of individuation. To me this truth seems clear and evident.

(13) The statement that matter is the principle of individuation does not mean that the identity of an individual consists in the identity of its matter. Thus it is not an objection against it that the matter of a man's body changes in the course of his life.[19]

I don't think that "principle of individuation" is an expression any counterpart of which is in Aristotle. So far as I know, the statement that according to Aristotle matter is the principle of individuation is based only on his saying that Callias and Socrates are "different in matter, for it is different" (sc. in each of them).

Clearly what is in question here is contemporaries. There is no question of saying that Professor Popper and Socrates differ materially. But Professor Popper and I, for example, differ in matter.

If I say this, I am not saying that Professor Popper is who he is because of *the* matter of which he is composed; so it is not a difficulty for me that he is materially in a state of flux. But of course if by "What is the principle of individuation?" you mean, or include, the question "What makes a man the same man at different times?" – then the answer "matter" is an absurd one. But as we are talking about Aristotle we have no right to take the question in that second sense at all. And I should say there were two quite different questions here which we ought not to mix up.

Aristotle writes very interestingly about nourishment and growth in the *De Generatione et Corruptione* I, 5: "Someone may wonder what it is that grows? Is it that to which something is added? For example, if someone grows in the leg, this gets bigger, but not that by means of which he grows, i.e. the food. Well, why don't *both* grow?"[20]

He goes on to say, isn't it because the substance of the one remains, and of the other not?[21] i.e. the food turns into the man. Further: ". . . flesh and bone and the rest are twofold, as is everything that has form in matter. For both the matter and the form are called flesh and bone. Thus it can be taken that every part grows – and grows by the accession of something – in respect

---

[19] This paper originally ended here. Professor Popper asked me to elaborate this section; but what follows reached him after he had completed his paper.

[20] *De Gen. et Corr.* I, 5, 321a30: ἀπορήσειε δ'ἄν τις καὶ τί ἐστι τὸ αὐξανόμενον, πότερον ᾧ προστίθεταί τι, οἶον εἰ τὴν κνήμην αὐξάνει, αὔτη μείζων, ᾧ δε αὐξάνει, ἡ τροφή, ου. διὰ τί δὴ οὖν οὐκ ἄμφω ηὔξηται;

[21] Ibid. 34: ἢ ὅτι τοῦ μὲν μένει ἡ ουσία, τοῦ δ' οὐ, οἶον τῆς τροφῆς;

of its form, but not in respect of its matter."[22] That is, we say that the *hand* grows, or the *flesh* or the *bone*. (Think of the ambiguity of the question "Is this the clay you were using last week?" – Aristotle would say that when we speak of 'this (bit of) clay' the word "clay" refers both to the form and to the matter.) Now matter can be added or taken away, but cannot be said to grow, for growth is *by* addition of matter. Thus it is that we use the term designating the *kind* of thing, to stand for the subject of growth. And then he adds: "It should be thought of like measuring water by the same measure. For something else keeps on becoming (the thing)."[23] That is, Aristotle compares the form to, say, the mile that we speak of when we say "this mile of river",[24] into which and out of which different water is constantly flowing. I find this a very illuminating comparison. It suggests the following picture to me: let us suppose that we could tag (as medical researchers speak of tagging) every particle of matter that went into Professor Popper – say by making everything that might go into him radio-active. After a few years had gone by wouldn't he be a reach of a stream of radio-active particles? I think of it literally quite pictorially: a stream of silvery particles with Professor Popper's outline drawn somewhere in the middle of it. Of course we mark 'this mile of river' by landmarks, as water does not change on entering and leaving it. But food and so on change substantially when they get into Professor Popper, so his form (the flesh and bone of a living man, to put it roughly) does the marking off; and corresponds to the mile of river.

I think this demonstrates quite clearly that if you mean anything Aristotelian by calling matter the principle of individuation, you do not mean that the identity of a person is the identity of the matter of which he is composed.

---

[22] Ibid. b19: σὰρξ καὶ ὀστοῦν καὶ ἕκαστον τῶν τοιούτων μορίων ἐστὶ διττόν, ὥσπερ καὶ τῶν ἄλλων τῶν ἐν ὕλῃ εἶδος ἐχόντων· καὶ γὰρ ἡ ὕλη λέγεται καὶ τὸ εἶδος σὰρξ καὶ ὀστοῦν. τὸ οὖν ὁτιοῦν μέρος αὐξάνεσθαι καὶ προσιόντος τινὸς κατὰ μὲν τὸ εἶδός ἐστιν ἐνδεχόμενον, κατὰ δε τὴν ὕλην οὐκ ἔστιν.

[23] Ibid. 24: δεῖ γὰρ νοῆσαι ὥσπερ εἴ τις μετροίη τῷ αὐτῷ μέτρῳ ὕδωρ· ἀεὶ γὰρ ἄλλο καὶ ἄλλο τὸ γινόμενον.

[24] I am indebted for this interpretation to Mr P. Geach, who threw it out almost as a joke in casual conversation: but I think it is obviously correct. I am grateful to him also for other help in preparing this paper.

7 Thought and Action in Aristotle

What is 'Practical Truth'?

Is Aristotle inconsistent in the different things he says about προαιρεσις, mostly translated "choice", in the different parts of the *Ethics*? The following seems to be a striking inconsistency. In Book III (1113a4) he says that what is "decided by deliberation" is chosen (το ἐκ της βουλης κριθεν προαιρετον ἐστιν), but he also often insists that the uncontrolled man, the ἀκρατης, does not *choose* to do what he does; that is to say, what he does in doing the kind of thing that he disapproves of, is not what Aristotle will call exercising choice; the uncontrolled man does not act from choice, ἐκ προαιρεσεως, or choosing, προαιρουμενος. However, in Book VI (1142b18) he mentions the possibility of a calculating uncontrolled man who will get what he arrived at by calculation, ἐκ του λογισμου τευξεται, and so will have deliberated correctly: ὀρθως ἐσται βεβουλευμενος. Thus we have the three theses: (1) choice is what is determined by deliberation; (2) what the uncontrolled man does *qua* uncontrolled, he does not choose to do; (3) the uncontrolled man, even when acting against his convictions, does on occasion determine what to do by deliberation.

Without a doubt the set of passages is inconsistent if we are to understand that any case of something being determined by deliberation at all is a case of choice, as seems to be suggested by the formulation "what is decided by deliberation is chosen".

If, then, Aristotle is consistent, perhaps his 'choice' is not *simply* determination by calculating or deliberating. There is some reason to think this; though he says that what is determined by deliberation (κριθεν ἐκ της βουλης) *is* chosen, we may say that the *context* shows that he himself has in mind a deliberation what to do with a view to one's ends, and that ends are things like being honoured, health, the life of virtue, or material prosperity, or enjoyment of knowledge, or sensual pleasure. The uncontrolled man, the ἀκρατης, is not one whose general object is, say, enjoying a life of sensual pleasure; he simply has the *particular* purpose of seducing his neighbour's wife.

On this view, we remove the inconsistency by saying that 'choice' is of something determined not just by any deliberation, but by deliberation how to obtain an object of one's *will* (βουλησις) rather than merely of one's *desire* (ἐπιθυμια): there will be a contrast here even for the ἀκολαστος, the licentious man. For *his* will is *to satisfy his desires, his sensual appetites*; and his decision to

---

From J. R. Bambrough (ed.), *New Essays on Plato and Aristotle* (London, 1965).

seduce his neighbour's wife, say, is a 'choice', as well as being an expression of his lusts, just because his end in life *is* to satisfy his lusts; this has to be shown before one can say that a man who is going after objects of 'desire' evilly, has a bad 'choice'.

Now – though I think this does represent Aristotle's view – an objection that strikes one is that people's 'ends' aren't in general nearly as definitely one thing or another as Aristotle makes out. *If* 'will' ($\beta o \upsilon \lambda \eta \sigma \iota \varsigma$) is simply the type of wanting ($\check{o} \rho \varepsilon \xi \iota \varsigma$) that one has in relation to one's final objective *in* what one is deliberately doing at any time, then there seems no objection to saying that the weak man at 1151a2 (the uncontrolled man who calculates how to get what tempts him, for he is surely a man of the weak rather than the impulsive type) has a *will* to seduce his neighbour's wife, or a will for the pleasure of it, at the time when he is cleverly reckoning how to do it. The fact that he has a bad conscience about it doesn't seem to be either here or there *for determining whether he is making that his aim* for the time being; but this fact, that he has a bad conscience about it, *is* just what makes him uncontrolled rather than licentious, $\mathring{a} \kappa \rho a \tau \eta \varsigma$ rather than $\mathring{a} \kappa \acute{o} \lambda a \sigma \tau o \varsigma$.

There is, however, another defence against the charge of inconsistency, which perhaps is not open to the objection that it requires an unrealistic idea of the clearcutness of people's ends. Not all deliberation is with a view to making a 'choice', forming a $\pi \rho o a \iota \rho \varepsilon \sigma \iota \varsigma$, where none has yet been made; some deliberation is with a view to executing a 'choice'. This is made clear at 1144a20; "Virtue makes one's choice right, but as for what has to be done for the sake of it, that doesn't belong to virtue but to another power – cleverness." ($\tau \eta \nu$ $\mu \varepsilon \nu$ $o \mathring{\upsilon} \nu$ $\pi \rho o a \iota \rho \varepsilon \sigma \iota \nu$ $\mathring{o} \rho \theta \eta \nu$ $\pi o \iota \varepsilon \iota$ $\mathring{\eta}$ $\mathring{a} \rho \varepsilon \tau \eta$. τo $\delta' \mathring{o} \sigma a$ $\mathring{\varepsilon} \kappa \varepsilon \iota \nu \eta \varsigma$ $\mathring{\varepsilon} \nu \varepsilon \kappa a$ $\pi \varepsilon \varphi \upsilon \kappa \varepsilon$ $\pi \rho a \tau \tau \varepsilon \sigma \theta a \iota$ $o \mathring{\upsilon} \kappa$ $\mathring{\varepsilon} \sigma \tau \iota$ $\tau \eta \varsigma$ $\mathring{a} \rho \varepsilon \tau \eta \varsigma$ $\mathring{a} \lambda \lambda'$ $\mathring{\varepsilon} \tau \varepsilon \rho a \varsigma$ $\delta \upsilon \nu a \mu \varepsilon \omega \varsigma$.)

But also in Book III Aristotle speaks of *trying* to do the thing that a deliberation has terminated in: "if it seems possible, they try to do it. Possible things are the things that *might* come about through us" (1112b26). So we might say that something that seems to be a way of achieving your end and to be possible may be decided upon; *that* you will do this (or at least will try) is a 'choice'; and now there may be further deliberation just how to manage that possible-seeming thing. Now in Book III there is no suggestion that wanting ($\check{o} \rho \varepsilon \xi \iota \varsigma$) of the more immediate means (adopted to execute the remoter means that have already been decided on) is not itself *also* a 'choice', $\pi \rho o a \iota \rho \varepsilon \sigma \iota \varsigma$. But if we are to reconcile the denial (which *also* occurs in Book III, 1111b14) that the uncontrolled man in acting, is *choosing* so to act ($\pi \rho o a \iota \rho o \upsilon \mu \varepsilon \nu o \varsigma$) with the account in Book VI of a calculating uncontrolled man, then we must say that when deliberation how to execute a decision terminates in an action – the man contrives a skilful approach to the woman – this will not be a case of 'choice' if the decision itself was not reached by deliberation.

Thus the passages in which Aristotle describes deliberation as going on till we have reached something we can do here and now, and describes 'choice' as being of what deliberation has reached, must not lead us to think that matter for a 'choice' has *only* been reached when there is no more room for deliberation of any kind.

On the other hand, just as the first defence left us wondering what Aristotle supposed a βούλησις, a case of 'will', to be, since apparently the pleasure sought by the uncontrolled man who calculates is not an object of his will; so this defence leaves us in the dark as to what a 'choice' is. We may well have thought we knew this; for 'what you can do here and now, which you have reached as a result of deliberating how to achieve an end' – the first cause (πρῶτον αἴτιον), the last thing in analysis and first in execution – did seem a relatively clear notion. But if, as must be admitted on the basis of the text, there is room for calculating how to execute a 'choice', then just where in the chain of deliberations from an end to the immediate thing that I can do without having to consider *how* to do it – just where in this chain does the first 'choice' come?

It must be admitted that Aristotle's account of deliberation (βούλευσις, or βουλή) often seems to fit deliberation about how to execute a decision, and in particular to fit technical deliberation, better than deliberation which is about the means here and now to 'living well in general' – πρὸς τὸ εὖ ζῆν ὅλως. It seems at its clearest when he is describing the doctor deliberating how to restore health by reducing the imbalance of humours by . . ., etc., But this is a piece of technical deliberation.

I am not saying that Aristotle so uses "προαίρεσις" ("choice") that the termination of a piece of technical deliberation isn't a 'choice'. On the contrary; that would, I think, be quite inconsistent with the treatment in Book III. But Book VI teaches us, as I think we might not have realized from Book III, that there is no such thing as a 'choice' which is *only* technical (I use "technical" to cover practical cleverness in bringing particular situations about, even when it's not strictly a technique that's in question). There is always, on Aristotle's view, another 'choice' behind a technical or purely executive one (1139b1–3). That is why he denies the name of "προαίρεσις", "choice", to the technical or executive decision, even though this is the fruit of deliberation, if that particular thing for the sake of which this decision is being made is not *itself* decided upon by deliberation.

To return to the weak, calculating, uncontrolled man, who disapproves of adultery but is tempted about his neighbour's wife: he gives way to the temptation and sets out to seduce her; then he calculates how best to do this and shows plenty of cleverness in his calculations. If he had been a licentious man, an ἀκόλαστος, the decision to seduce her would have been a 'choice', and the volition to perform each of the steps that he reckoned would enable him to succeed would in turn each have been a 'choice' too. For the decision to seduce this woman was simply the particular application of his general policy of pursuing sensual enjoyment. But although the uncontrolled man perhaps reckons how to proceed – once he has given way to the temptation to go after this woman – in exactly the same way as the licentious man, his volitions in performing the steps that he calculates will enable him to succeed are not 'choices'. (Aristotle, of course, does not set up a word for 'volition' as I have been using it.) So we have to say that the uncontrolled man carries out a deliberation how to execute what would have been a 'choice' if he had been an ἀκόλαστος; this, however, is something for which Aristotle has no regular name – for he has no general use of a psychological verb or abstract noun corresponding to "*ἑκούσιον*" (usually translated "voluntary") as "*προαιρεῖσθαι*" ("choose"), "*προαίρεσις*" ("choice"), correspond to "*προαιρετόν*" ("chosen"). Of course he regards the uncontrolled man as acting voluntarily. When he describes this man as calculating cleverly, he says he will get what he 'proposes' (*προτίθεται*); and this verb expresses a volition, or perhaps rather an intention. Aristotle ought, we may say, to have seen that he was here employing a key concept in the theory of action, but he did not do so; the innocent unnoticeable verb he uses receives no attention from him.

Let us return to the point that a technical 'choice' is never the only 'choice' that is made by the man who makes it. The definition of 'choice' as ὄρεξις βουλευτική – deliberative wanting – would not at first sight seem to justify this. The calculating uncontrolled man choosing means of seduction – he wants them, surely, i.e. has an ὄρεξις for them, and this is a result of deliberation. However, there is – what may give us pause in making this criticism – a puzzling remark in that passage in Book VI (1139a17–b13) where Aristotle devotes most discussion to this definition of 'choice'. He says ". . . choice does not exist without intellect and judgement, *nor yet without* moral character". (. . . οὔτ᾽ ἄνευ νοῦ καὶ διανοίας οὔτ᾽ ἄνευ ἠθικῆς ἐστιν ἕξεως ἡ προαίρεσις.) That sentence, in fact, starts with the word "*διο*" – "That is why". It is puzzling, because while the previous sentences give ample grounds for saying that choice involves intelligence, they don't seem to give any ground for saying that it involves moral character. However, the succeeding sentence starts "For" – so perhaps we should look for the explanation there first. "For doing well, and its opposite, does not exist without judgement and character." (εὐπραξία γὰρ καὶ τὸ ἐναντίον ἐν πράξει ἄνευ διανοίας καὶ ἤθους οὐκ ἐστιν.) That does not seem to help us much. A little farther on, however, he tells us "The end, absolutely speaking, is not anything one *makes*, but something one *does*. For doing well is the end, and that is the object of the wanting (ἡ δ᾽ ὄρεξις τούτου). That is why choice is appetitive (ὀρεκτική) intelligence or intelligent wanting."

This brings us back to our first defence; namely, that something is only a 'choice' if it is of means to the objects of a man's 'will' (βούλησις); hence, however much calculation may have gone into determining it, if it is of what is only a means to the objects of a man's ἐπιθυμίαι, his 'desires', then unless his 'will' in life *is* to satisfy these desires (as holds of the licentious man) it is not a 'choice'. Thus the second defence resolves into the first. The second defence was that since some deliberation is done with a view to executing a 'choice', something may be reached as a result of deliberation even when the significant decision what to do has already been made; and if this has *not* been made by deliberation (κριθεν ἐκ της βουλης), then it was not a 'choice', and the results of deliberations how to execute it won't be 'choices' either. Well, the question whether the significant decision is reached by deliberation seems to reduce to the question whether it is made with a view to the objects of the man's 'will' (βουλησις). Now our question about this was: what does Aristotle suppose 'will' (βουλησις) to be? Why, we asked, shouldn't we say that the uncontrolled man has a 'will' for the pleasure he hopes to obtain from seducing his neighbour's wife? The answer we get suggested by the passage in Book VI is: the uncontrolled man is not prepared to say: "This is my idea of good work (εὐπραξια), this is the kind of life I want." Whereas, of course, that is the attitude of the licentious man, the ἀκολαστος: a life spent doing such things is his idea of a well-spent life – and a fig for moral virtue. It is not that the licentious man thinks licentiousness is moral virtue; what he thinks is rather that this is a good way to carry on. "One should pursue the present pleasure", δει το παρον ἠδυ διωκειν, doesn't mean: it's virtuous, or morally obligatory, to do that – but: that's the thing to do!

Now, why can't one have 'choice' without moral character of some sort? I think Aristotle does not explain this, beyond saying that 'doing well', 'a good way of carrying on' is the end of any 'choice'; i.e. any sort of decision which does not have in view what one thinks of as a good way of proceeding in one's life, does *not* qualify to be a 'choice'.

His thesis, then, clearly is that there is no such thing as your acting with εὐπραξια, 'doing well', in view unless you have some sort of moral character, virtuous or vicious. Now, how is this? Let us imagine some cases.

Someone thinks that it is a good sort of life always to get the better of people by tricking them, taking them in, defrauding them; to do that is to be strong and not soft and not a sucker oneself, and to get the best of whatever's going; whereas the honest man is weak and soft and a fool, and always gets the worst of things. A particular decision to cheat X will be a 'choice' of something here and now which he makes for the sake of doing well as he conceives it.

Another case: someone thinks that he will do well if he spends his life in scientific research; to do this he must have leisure; to get the money for his living expenses he does a disgraceful but not time-consuming thing: one great fraud.

These are two rather different types of case; however, in both of them it would be natural enough to say that the man is described as having a sort of moral character. On Aristotle's view, a character exists only when there is an habitual performance of the typical acts of that character. Now I have described the cases so that the men's ends are clear, but I have put in only one act for each. The first case is not credibly described on the supposition that there is only one such act. This one act with a view to this sort of 'doing well' – what is supposed to have preceded it? Has he done things of the same sort, but not done them under any such conception? under what conception, then? – say in obedience to a mentor, or attracted by the particular gains of each action? Very well; but what is to make us call this the first act done with a view to that sort of 'doing well'? It is not enough for the agent to have those thoughts; suppose he had them on just one occasion – that would not show that he was acting so as to 'do well' in that kind of way, only that he had indulged in a certain picture of his actions. Only if they are the thoughts which come to habitually inspire those actions shall we be able to say: that is his end, that is his idea of a good way of going on. If, on the other hand, he had not done any actions of the sort before, then still more one would want plenty of actions performed under the influence of his new thoughts before one could recognize one as done with a view to this sort of 'doing well' rather than as, say, an experiment in wrongdoing.

The other case is different; here the single act which is to be the object of a choice is not the kind of act which the agent supposes to be the way to spend his life well. If the agent had never done any scientific research or study at all, then the description of the case would be suspect. Either it would be non-sense, or it would be a description of someone under a fantastic illusion. Perhaps it is possible to conceive something as the activity you aim to spend your life at even though you never do it at all, even in a feeble and elementary fashion. But then either it would have to be something you could understand without doing it (like riding horses, say), or you could only want the name, no doubt with some piece of imagination attached – as if, e.g., someone who had never learnt any mathematics wanted to become a mathematician because of the expression on the face of a mathematician he knew, and had no other conception of a good way of spending his life: that was it, for him. This would rather be a lunatic obsession than a conception of a certain sort of doing well as the end.

If, then, 'choice' is only of those things which are done as means to 'doing well', we may concede that Aristotle is right in saying that it does not occur without moral character, i.e. without good or bad habitual action. But there is no reason to say that the action which is the subject of 'choice' must itself be the act of a virtue or a vice. That will only be so where the objects of 'choice' are (in Greenwood's phrase) constitutive means towards the (putative) good way of going on. In the second case I described, the fraudulent act was a productive means; and if the man did not perform other fraudulent acts, this act would not mean that he was a fraudulent man – i.e. that he had the vice of being fraudulent.

The notion of 'choice' as conceived by Aristotle, his προαιρεσις, is a very peculiar one. I used to think it spurious. If it had been a winner, like some other Aristotelian concepts, would not "prohaeretic" be a word as familiar to us as "practical" is?

At any rate, 'choice' cannot do all the work Aristotle wants to make it do. The uncontrolled man who has further intentions in doing what he does, whose actions are deliberate, although the deliberation is in the interests of a desire which conflicts with what he regards as doing well – to describe his action we need a concept (our 'intention') having to do with will or appetition: not just ἐπιθυμια, 'desire', for that may be only a feeling.

Aristotle talks as if 'desire' were a force (1147a34), but this is only a metaphor. He will have it that if one acts against one's convictions, one's judgement has always failed in some way under the influence of 'desire' or some other passion. One fails to know or remember either the last premise or, possibly, the conclusion. There are such cases. For example, a man who disapproves of adultery may fail to find out something which he easily could have found out, and so may commit adultery through culpable ignorance of a particular premise: "This woman, whom I have picked up at a party, is someone's wife" – his failure to find out being explained by his passion. And similarly for failure to get or keep clear before one's mind already known facts, with their implications for action in view of one's ends; and for lies one may tell inwardly or outwardly when one wants to do wrong. But Aristotle writes as if these were the only cases of doing what you believe is wrong. He apparently cannot admit the case where a person forms a perfectly clear-headed intention of acting contrary to his convictions. On one interpretation the trouble always concerns one of the particular premises; on another, Aristotle allows a case where the sinner is clear about all these, but then fails to draw the conclusion; at most he draws it verbally, without knowledge of what he is saying.

The usual explanations of this are that Aristotle was a Greek, that he was still under Plato's influence, etc. No doubt there is something in that; particularly when he restricts the explanation "he repeats the thing, but it's just babble like a drunk man reciting Empedocles" to the particular premise: or possibly to that and the conclusion. It is, surely, an explanation far better suited to enunciation of the universal premise, say: "No one should commit adultery" or "It is disgraceful to get very drunk", by the man who is about to do it. Aristotle explicitly wants to exempt knowledge of general principles from 'being dragged about like a slave'.

However, I suspect that he was also influenced by his own conception of practical reasoning. To set out the form of practical reasoning is to set out the form of deliberation (βουλευσις). If it is all made explicit (as of course it hardly would be in real life, since one does not need to advert to the obvious) its formal character becomes quite clear. You have a set of premises starting with a universal one to the effect that a kind of thing A is, say, profitable for a kind of being B, and proceeding through intermediate premises like "Cs are As" and "a C can be obtained by a procedure D" and "a procedure D can be carried out by doing E", together with another premise to the effect that you are (or someone whose profit is your concern is) a B; and if the action E is something that you can do, then it is clear that the conclusion of this reasoning is for you to do E. But let us consider what this means. Does it mean that if you have embarked on the reasoning you *must* do E? Aristotle seems to have thought so. At least he thought you must do E unless something prevented you – the something might be the drive of 'desire', ἐπιθυμια, *against* doing E. When making this point, he often gave examples of practical syllogisms in which there is a certain necessity about the conclusion – "It is necessary to taste everything sweet, and this is sweet" (1147a29); "Every man must walk, and I am a man"; "Now no man must walk, and I am a man". The last two examples come from the *Movement of Animals*, Chapter VII. The man does the thing in question (walks or halts) at once, if not prevented from walking in the one case, or forced to walk in the other. There are two features suggesting the necessity of the conclusion – the gerundive form, and the type of universality in the premise.

> Every man has got to walk
> I am a man
> I have got to walk

is a formally valid deductive argument – I will call such an argument a proof-syllogism. I mean that it is a proof of the conclusion, if only the premises are true. Now Aristotle had special ideas about proof, so he would not have agreed to say what I have just said. "Every man has got to walk" is not a changeless truth, so he would have said this is not apodeictic (see, e.g., 1140a33–5). Disregarding this let us merely note the formal validity of the reasoning as a deduction. Further, let us grant that if I agree to the premises and therefore to the conclusion, and say "I have got to walk", speaking quite seriously, it would be queer of me not to walk, if nothing prevented me.

Now let us look at another example from the *Movement of Animals*:

> I need a covering,
> A cloak is a covering,
> I need a cloak;
> I must make what I need,
> I need a cloak,
> I must make a cloak.

The conclusion, that a cloak must be made, Aristotle says, *is* an action: το συμπερασμα το ιματιον ποιητεον πραξις εστι. So here is a 'choice'. But, he goes on, action has a starting-point – and so he sketches the reasoning with a view to execution of the 'choice': "If there's to be a cloak, first such and such is needed, and if such and such, so and so" (εἰ ἱματιον ἐσται, ἀναγκη τοδε πρωτον, εἰ δε τοδε, τοδε), and this last the man does at once. Now it is hard to tell whether Aristotle reflected that "I need a cloak" is not a formally valid deductive conclusion from "I need a covering and a cloak is a covering". The fact that it is not, is, I should contend, no criticism of the syllogism as a piece of practical reasoning. But it is possible that if he had been challenged about this, he would have said one could amend the syllogism by putting in that a cloak was the best covering or the easiest to make or something of that sort (cf. *Nicomachean Ethics*, 1112b16). For he is marked by an anxiety to make practical reasoning out to be as like as possible to speculative reasoning. "They work just the same", he says in the *Movement of Animals* (ἐοικε παραπλησιως συμβαινειν), and seems to be referring to a necessitation of the conclusion. But you do not get this where various ways of obtaining the end are possible.

A further sign is that when he is looking at practical syllogism in this light – as necessarily yielding the conclusion – his examples of the first universal premises always go "It's needed", "It's expedient", "such and such a kind of being ought to do such and such a kind of thing". He wants a "must" in the conclusion in the verbalized form in which he gives it in the *Movement of Animals*, though each time he gives the conclusion he adds – "and that's an action". But when he is not talking about this automatic-machine aspect of the practical syllogism – which he is keen on because he thinks it helps to make it clear how the syllogism κινει, how it sets the human animal in motion – then we have such a universal premise as "Heavy waters are unwholesome". Here the *De Anima* formulation (of a doctrine also expressed in the *Nicomachean Ethics* at 1140b16, though not so clearly) that the starting-point of the whole business is what you want (the ἀρχη is the ὀρεκτον) can come into play. And we may remark that there are two possible conclusions of the reasoning about heavy waters, according as you want to be healthy or not. That, of course, sounds absurd; but let the universal be "Strong alkalis are deadly poison", and it is easy to spell out the practical reasoning of the suicide. Aristotle recognizes this two-way possibility at *Metaphysics* IX, 1046b5–8.

It looks as if, in his enthusiasm for making practical reasoning like theoretical and explaining its power to set one in motion (aided, no doubt, by his own picture of proof and by the Platonic conception of sin as error, which he did not entirely shake off), Aristotle did not notice some significant features of his discovery; the fact that though it is perfectly correct to call practical reasoning 'reasoning', and though some practical syllogisms are also (in my sense) proof syllogisms, i.e. are entailments, in general practical syllogisms have a different form from proof syllogisms.

Consider:

Owning a Launderette would make me wealthy.
There is scope for opening a Launderette in such-and-such a place

and so on down to where I might get going. This is practical reasoning, and given all the premises it is a formal matter what the conclusion is, in the form 'so I'll . . .'. Whether, if it is I who have put out the syllogism, I *draw* the conclusion, depends on whether I actively aim at being rich and am working out this one of the many possibilities with a view to action – I might be doing it idly, or as an academic example. If by a practical syllogism you mean – as Aristotle did (*De Anima*, 433a15) – one that terminates in action, and the purpose of which is to act, then this won't be practical; but if you mean a *type* of reasoning – i.e. reasoning reaching from a general sort of objective to something one can choose to do here and now – then it will be practical (St Thomas would call it "theoretical *de practicis*" (*Summa Theologica*, 1a. 14, art.

16c.). In general, people would not trouble to work such things out except with a view to action.

We have seen two strands in Aristotle's thought. First there is the explanation of how the human being is set in motion by thought, and second there is the idea of the thing wanted as the starting-point for such thought. For the first he seems to have wanted not only a necessity in the connections which is not always present in practical reasonings, but also a compulsiveness about the universal premise, a 'must' about it: that is, it seems he wanted a universal premise acceptance of which implies intellectual acknowledgement of it as the guide to action. The need for necessity in the connections can fairly be discounted. Then we can happily combine the two strands by postulating at the back of all these premises a first premise to the effect that only such-and-such is doing well, is happiness or blessedness, 'the good for man'. Aristotle's grand universal premise is that blessedness is activity in accordance with virtue, especially intellectual virtue. The argument for this as the true premise is the *Nicomachean Ethics* itself. If the truth of this premise is acknowledged, then it is itself acknowledged as the ultimate guide to action. For blessedness, or doing well, is the end that anyone must have so far as he has a rational end, that is to say so far as he has 'will', i.e. the kind of wanting that belongs in the rational part, at all (cf. *De Anima*, 432b5–7).

Here we touch on the difference between Aristotle and Hume. Hume's doctrine that reason is inert, that for considerations to lead to any action a sentiment, a passion, is required may be compared to Aristotle's "It is not reason as such that sets in motion; but reason which is with a view to something and is practical" (1139a36). Aristotle's 'will' will then be a 'calm passion' in Hume's terminology. But they disagree about the applicability of the descriptions "in accordance with reason" and "not in accordance with reason" to actions and wants.

I suggest that the idea of rational wanting should be explained in terms of what is wanted being wanted *qua* conducive to or part of 'doing well', or blessedness. If one admits that what one wants is no good, but still one wants it, it is, in Aristotle's conception, merely the object of a passion; when the thing that one so wants is a pleasure, though it is no good (like smoking in some people's view) then one is being led simply by 'desire', ἐπιθυμια. For though what constitutes blessedness is necessarily utterly pleasant, it isn't something one wants because it is a pleasure even though it should be no good; on the contrary, it is the object of will as the best possible thing for a human being, being the actualization of his rational part and an actualization that is an end, not a means.

For as seeing can be seen to be what the eye is for, so understanding – the enjoyment of the truth – can be seen to be what the mind is for. But here we must note a certain split in Aristotle's thought. For the highest blessedness he thought of as something divine, which we should grasp at to the poor extent that we can – taking the side of and imitating the immortal. He coins a word for what we should do, namely "to immortalize" (ἀθανατιζειν 1177b33), sounding like an echo of "to Medize" which means to be on the side of and imitate the Persian. But he acknowledges that in the ordinary course of life for most people 'doing well' amounts to something more mundane: a successful and honourable conduct of life, the heart of which is, if one judges rightly, action in accordance with *moral* virtue.

Apart from being ruled by passion (this is what I want, even if it is no good) 'doing well' is what anyone wants in some obscure and indeterminate way. One could call it that part of blessedness for which one's own action is essential. Aristotle's unrealistic conception of the clearcutness of people's ends seems on investigation not to be so bad as it looked. For the many objectives that are no good are allowed for in his thought. The assumption of clearcutness is the assumption that people generally know what they count as 'doing well' – i.e. that they definitely so count being rich or being famous or the life of knowledge.

My eventual goal has been to expound the concept of 'practical truth' and the discussion of *Nicomachean Ethics*, Book VI, Chapter II on 'choice'. I will start from 1139a21. "What affirmation and negation are in judgement, pursuit and avoidance are in desire." That is, one can say "yes" or "no" both to a statement and to a proposal. Suppose, then, that the statement should say that doing such and such is 'doing well'. There is the "yes" in judgement and the "yes" in the will, meaning that one wants to do that sort of thing. For to characterize it as 'doing well' is *eo ipso* to propose it as an object of 'will' – to put it up as a candidate for 'will', βουλησις.

"So," Aristotle goes on, "since moral virtue is a disposition of one's choice, while choice is deliberated wanting, these things show that the judgement must be true and the wanting right, if the choice is to be sound, and the one must say and the other pursue the same thing." We may remark that the one must say and the other pursue the same thing if there is to be any 'choice' at all, sound or unsound. So far we have only mentioned the judgement on what ευπραξια, doing well, is. A false judgement on this necessarily means that if there is a 'choice' at all the wanting in it is wrong. To make this clear, imagine a worldling's idea of doing well. If the worldly man has any wants that are right, they don't occur in his 'choices'. Any 'choice' that he makes, since in 'choice' the wanting goes after what the judgement declares to be doing well, must involve wrong wanting.

Can the judgement be false at a lower level than one's idea of doing well, without the wanting being wrong if they are in accord? Suppose the man has judged truly, as Aristotle would say and as I want to say, that to act justly is necessary for doing well, but falsely that justice would be done by dividing all the goods available in the country into equal shares according to the number of the population and assigning each share to one person by picking name and number of share out of a hat; or that it is justice for a poor man to be punished for assaulting a rich one, but not vice versa. I am not speaking of particular procedures, but of judgements about what *sort* of procedures are just.

It appears to me that *only* when we get to questions where it is difficult to know the truth, or questions as to facts which the agent can't be expected to have found out, is there any chance for the wanting of what is judged a means to doing well to be right when the judgement itself is wrong. This then will be why Aristotle said in Book III (1110b31) that ignorance in choice, ἡ ἐν τῇ προαιρέσει ἄγνοια, is the cause not of involuntariness but of scoundrelism. He himself laid down the rule about difficulty at 1113b33–1114a2.

We now approach the great question: what does Aristotle mean by "practical truth"? He calls it the good working, or the work, of practical judgement; and practical judgement is judgement of the kind described, terminating in action. It is practical truth when the judgements involved in the formation of the 'choice' leading to the action are all true; but the practical truth is not the truth of those *judgements*. For it is clearly that 'truth in agreement with right desire' (ἀλήθεια ὁμολογως ἔχουσα τῇ ὀρέξει τῇ ὀρθῇ) (1139a30), which is spoken of as the good working (εὖ), or the work (ἔργον), of practical intelligence. That is brought about – i.e. made true – by action (since the description of what he does is made true by his doing it), provided that a man forms and executes a good 'choice'. The man who forms and executes an evil 'choice' will also make true *some* description of what he does. He will secure, say, if he is competent, that such and such a man has his eyes put out or his hands cut off, that being his judgement of what it is just to do. But his description "justice performed" of what he has done will be a lie. He, then, will have produced practical falsehood.

"Since everything that is done about them is false, how should these be gods?" – The notion of *truth or falsehood in action* would quite generally be countered by the objection that "true" and "false" are senseless predicates as applied to what is done. If I am right there is philosophy to the contrary in Aristotle. And if, as I should maintain, the idea of *descriptions under which* what is done is voluntary is integral to his notion of action (*praxis*), then these predicates apply to actions (*praxeis*) strictly and properly, and not merely by an extension and in a way that ought to be explained away.

Part Two

*Medieval and
Modern Philosophers*

8 Necessity and Truth

What is known must be true; hence it readily appears that only the necessarily true can be known. This is probably one root of the Greek conception that knowledge is of the changelessly true. Nowadays an undergraduate early learns to criticize the passage from "What is known is necessarily true" to "Only the necessarily true is known"; the former is correct only in the sense that if something is not true then my certainty that it is the case is – necessarily – not knowledge; and from this nothing follows placing any restriction on the objects of knowledge.

One is likely to learn this criticism in connection with Plato's doctrine that only supra-sensible forms were objects of knowledge properly so-called, and Aristotle's doctrine that the sphere of knowledge was only: the kind of thing that cannot be otherwise. The appearance of the first volumes – of a set of sixty – of a new translation of the *Summa Theologiae* (sometimes called the *Summa Theologica*) of St Thomas Aquinas prompts one to ponder St Thomas's attitude to this question.

We find it presented in him in a heightened form: must not God's knowledge be only of what is necessarily true? – so that either there is no contingency about the future, or God does not know all that is to come (1a, 14, art. 13). St Thomas is indeed partly caught in the trap of argument with which we opened. He escapes from it – without fully realizing this – by an appeal to the distinction between necessity *de re* and necessity *de dicto*, as we did. For that is what our argument was, though the point may be obscured by the fact that the *res* in question, the things that are known, appear themselves as *dicta*, such as *that so-and-so will win the next election* (known only to God) or *that I shall not find that pot of coffee at my elbow too hot to drink* (known well to me). The compatibility between the contingency (non-necessity) of these known *res* and the necessity *de dicto* "What is known is true" is the right way out of the trap . . . But one goes straight back into it like this: must not the fact of the knowledge of such a contingency itself be equally contingent? That is to say, must it not always be capable of turning out false, that such-and-such a way for the future to turn out is known to be the way it will turn out? For, being contingent, this thing may not happen.

Many might want to accept this so far as concerns human knowledge, and so hold that there is after all no escape from the trap. St Thomas was stopped from accepting it for divine knowledge, which thus, as so often, assumes the position as it were of a pure sample in a thought-experiment. (As when Professor Ayer in his youth, in spite of *Language, Truth and Logic*, was observed rocking on the floor in a discussion and exclaiming "God doesn't

A revised version of the article that appeared in the *Times Literary Supplement* (14 February 1965).

know any negative facts!") In this case we come up with the result: If *it was known that p* is unalterably true (because a past fact) still it does not follow that *necessarily p* is true even when the truth of *p* follows with logical necessity from *it was known that p*. This appears to St Thomas far too paradoxical for human knowledge; he therefore infers that humans cannot know future contingents and makes a suspiciously facile use of Boethius' definition of eternity as *interminabilis vitae tota simul et perfecta possessio* (the complete possession all at once of endless life) in order to compare God's knowledge of future contingents to our knowledge of present facts. Our own knowledge of future events is only in their present causes; when these do not absolutely necessitate their effects, so that the effects are contingent, he thinks we cannot know them. But, we might argue on his own principles, what causes in the world cannot conceivably be tampered with, at least by divine power? Thus we can know nothing of the future.

St Thomas surely did not need to adopt these devices: he had put his hand on the solution in the distinction between the true *de dicto* necessity *what is known is true* and the false *de re* pronouncement *what is known is necessary*. And this can be applied to human knowledge no less than to divine. Knowledge is not restricted to what could not imaginably turn out mistaken: given that there are not more specific grounds for refusing the title "knowledge" to my claim that something is true, it is sufficient that the claim does not turn out mistaken. It may be that I can conceive circumstances that would prove me wrong; that does not show that I may be wrong. G. E. Moore was labouring to this conclusion in his last years, but – he felt – could not get it out satisfactorily.

"But," someone says, "if the coffee can turn out to be hot after all, then you may be wrong in saying it won't." Well, if it turns out hot I shall grant I did not know it would not; but I say it will not. And why should its being possible to imagine my being wrong, prove me not to know, in the case where I turn out to have been right? "But that makes any proof that you know capable of refutation, if on examination the coffee turns out hot." So it is: I cannot have a better proof that I know the coffee will not be hot, than I could have that the coffee will not be hot: and no proof of that would withstand its actually turning out to be hot. "But the reasons for present knowledge must be present reasons, and if these do not prove the future contingent assertion, the alleged knowledge is not knowledge!" This is again the requirement that the object of knowledge be necessary. None of this shows me not to know now. To adapt to our own purposes the last sentence of Aquinas's article:

> Since the expression "known" refers to the actual context of knowing, the thing that is known, even though it is known now, can be characterized in itself in a way in which it cannot be characterized *qua* belonging to the actual context of knowing (namely, as future): in the same way, materiality is attributed to a stone as it is in itself, but not as an object of thought. (1a, 14, 13ad 3)

Thomas's own consideration would put "contingent" where I put "future". Thus he says that *qua* object of God's knowledge the future *is* necessary, when in itself it is not. The comparison with the immateriality of material things in thought shows that the divine mind does not *take* the future to be necessary. But the conception seems too difficult; it has to be eked out by that of a point of view outside time. The contingency of the future events in themselves is said to derive from the contingency of their proximate causes, which I take to mean the non-necessitation by those causes.

He is dismissive of a number of logical suggestions, such as that "God knew this future contingent thing would happen" turns out contingent on analysis. These dismissals are intriguingly obscure; the whole passage is in any case immensely interesting.

It belonged to the temper of St Thomas's time and to his own not to profess originality but rather to agree with previous authorities as much as possible. And there was a long tradition, limiting human knowledge to the necessary. Accordingly we find St Thomas maintaining this opinion. Of itself this would not exclude history from being known since Aristotle held that the past is necessary; but St Thomas goes farther than this in his adherence to the Greek conception of knowledge; in the field of speculative reason, he says everything derives from some first, indemonstrable principles which are known of themselves. Indeed in at least one place (1a 2ae, 94, 2c) we find him saying that everything in this sphere is "founded upon" the principle of contradiction.

These views put forward in this manner certainly appear archaic; but, on further reflection, are they so after all? Indeed if one speaks in the manner of Plato of "objects of knowledge" and "objects of opinion" it will be replied by everyone that these things do not have to differ in their objects. But up to a short while ago it was extremely common in effect to distinguish such objects: did not Professor Ayer, in common with many others, teach that all that was certain was either a truth of logic or an expression of immediate experience like "I am imagining a red circle" – all else being at best merely probable? These doctrines indeed are now not so much taught; but it is a standard method to test any philosophical assertion – e.g. "Emotion always has an object", "A cause must be prior to its effect" – by considering whether a counter-example to it can be conceived without contradiction. Contradiction indeed may have to be rather generously conceived: not every inconceivability can be displayed as of the form "both thus and not thus", where the two occurrences of the word "thus" are replaced by the same term. Sometimes an inconceivability seems irreducibly of the kind where the two "thuses" receive different substitutions as in "both coloured and not extended" or – to take examples claimed by Aquinas – "both a human being and lacking any potentiality for laughter", "both an existent by sharing in existence and uncaused" (1a, 3, 6c and 44, 1ad).

Thus what might at first seem archaic turns out on reflection to conform to very general philosophical practice: philosophic understanding, we tend to think, concerns what must be so. Or if philosophic understanding is achieved by a successful delineation of concepts, of how they happen to be in this our – or any human – culture, then our great interest is to note what could not be supposed changed about a concept without quite changing what we are talking about in using it, as we change the propositions of geometry by changing from one geometrical system to another – what, that is, belongs to what St Thomas calls the *ratio formalis obiecti*. Such a phrase, it will be clear, is difficult to explain or to translate very directly, unless one is to employ the gobbledegook of mere transverbalization – the original technique of the Latin translations of Aristotle and the first English translation of St Thomas. The present translation is very different; one translator offers us what is rather an explanatory commentary than a translation, a course it is difficult to approve. But the fact that it is now not so difficult to explain such phrases marks some change in philosophy. We are nowadays in some ways closer to the ancient and the medievals than we are to, say, Kant and Hegel. There are doubtless many points which go together to form this situation: but if the reviewer were challenged to name what most strikes him he would point to the eclipse in recent philosophy of the notion of "the given" and the manner of the current gradual redeparture from atomistic conceptions. Asked what was given, a present-day English speaking philosopher would be very likely to say 'the lot'. We start *mediis in rebus*; our philosophic activity is one of describing and clarifying this milieu to ourselves. What we believe to exist we credit and what we do not believe to exist we discredit, not on grounds of any *a priori* conception of knowledge, language, meaning and truth. On what grounds, then? Why do we not, if we do not, believe in the Evil Eye? – in which St Thomas, like many present-day Neapolitans, did believe, giving a rationalistic account of the phenomenon (1a, 117, 3, ad 2). It is to be feared that the reason is often, largely: because the people around us do not. But perhaps we are not all entirely lazy: there is a great deal of work to do before we can face such questions. We want to get clear about the concepts we habitually use before we trust ourselves as philosophers to use them for purposes beyond our immediate ken. So we accept common views, or remain in views not arrived at by philosophy while we work at concepts; and it is noteworthy that concepts of experiencing are only some – equal citizens, no more – among those that we want to understand. The logical features of concepts, which we want to describe, are such as to make us need tools of philosophic description not always unlike those used by a medieval philosopher. We can often see what he was at where our great-grandfathers – sometimes even our fathers – could see nothing but useless subtleties and distinctions. The sorting out by Aquinas of the *de re* and *de dicto* necessities confounded in 'what is known is necessarily true' is something a present-day English philosopher can appreciate.

The retreat from atomism, though it is easy not to realize this, is far more difficult to carry out successfully than might appear. Indeed it is well established now that we cannot regard the emotions as merely contingently connected with the kind of objects they have and the aims they tend to make us have. And it seems equally clear that thoughts are characterized by what they are of, with no substantive being of their own; but how this is so is so intensely obscure that one surveys the obscurities of the scholastic *esse intelligibile*, whose actuality is the same thing as the actual occurrence of a thought of such-and-such, with a not totally unfavourable eye. The medieval concept of intentional existence, called 'intentional inexistence' by the scholastically trained philosopher Brentano, may even be making a come-back, a reappearance in modern dress. But these matters are still very dark.

9   Hume and Julius Caesar

I

Section IV of Part III of Book I of the *Treatise* is a doubly unusual piece of philosophical writing for Hume. Read very casually, all seems uncommonly smooth and acceptable. A little attention, and it collapses. Revision is incontrovertibly needed to secure coherence. The needed revision then reveals the position as incredible.

The topic is our belief in matters falling outside our own experience and memory:

> When we infer effects from causes, we must establish the existence of these causes . . . either by an immediate perception of our memory or senses, or by an inference from other causes; which causes we must ascertain in the same manner either by a present impression, or by an inference from their causes and so on, until we arrive at some object which we see or remember. 'Tis impossible for us to carry on our inferences *in infinitum*, and the only thing that can stop them, is an impression of the memory or senses, beyond which there is no room for doubt or enquiry. (Selby-Bigge's edition, pp. 82–3)

Now this is a credible account of a kind of *prognosis* from what is seen or remembered. That once noted, what must be our astonishment on observing that in illustration Hume invites us

> To chuse any point of history, and consider for what reason we either believe or reject it. Thus we believe that Caesar was kill'd in the senate-house[1] on the *ides* of *March*; and that because this fact is established on the unanimous testimony of historians . . . Here are certain characters and letters . . . the signs of certain ideas; and these ideas were either in the minds of such as were immediately present at that action; or they were deriv'd from . . . testimony . . . and that again from another testimony . . . 'till we arrive at . . . eye witnesses and spectators of the event. 'Tis obvious all this chain of argument or connexion of causes and effects is at first founded on those characters or letters, which are seen or remember'd.

This is not to infer effects from causes, but rather causes from effects. We must, then, amend: "When we infer effects from causes *or* causes from effects", etc. For historical belief:

> When we infer causes from effects, we must establish the existence of those effects, either by perception or by inference from other effects; which effects we must

---

[1] Stickling for accuracy, I believe this is false, if by 'senate-house' Hume meant to indicate a building. The Senate was not meeting in the senate-house.

From *Analysis*, 34, 1 (1973).

ascertain in the same manner by a present impression or by an inference from their effects and so on, until we arrive at an object which we see or remember.

For Hume, the relation of cause and effect is the one bridge by which to reach belief in matters beyond our present impressions or memories. (That is why the Section "On the idea, or belief" is in the middle of the Part which we would think of as the Part on cause.) But also, cause and effect are inferentially symmetrical.

The historical example is an inference of the original cause, the killing of Caesar, from its remote effect, the present perception of certain characters or letters. The inference goes through a chain of effects of causes which are effects of causes, etc. What is its starting-point? It is natural to say the starting-point is the present perception.

But that cannot be a sufficient exegesis! For what on this account has become of the argument that we cannot go on *in infinitum*? The end of the chain is now the death of Caesar or the perception of its eyewitnesses, not our perception. But it has to be our perception. What is in question isn't a chain nailed at both ends, but a cantilever.

The impossibility of running up with our inferences *in infinitum* was not occasioned by our incapacity or exhaustion. The chain of inference has to stop or else "there wou'd be no belief nor evidence. And this actually is the case with all *hypothetical* arguments; there being in them neither any present impressions, nor belief of a real existence". (ibid.)

"'Tis impossible for us to carry on our inference *in infinitum*" means: *the justification of the grounds of our inferences cannot go on in infinitum.* Where we have chains of belief on grounds believed on grounds . . . we must come to belief which we do not base on grounds. The argument here is that there must *be* a starting point of the inference to the original cause, not that inference must terminate. Indeed, one reason why this passage of Hume's seems fairly ordinary and acceptable at first sight is, that he strikes one as just making this point, together with the one that the starting-point must be perception.

Does our original amendment "When we infer effects from causes, or causes from effects . . ." still stand? Yes, it must. But Hume is arguing not merely that we must have a starting-point, but that we must *reach* a starting-point in the justification of these inferences. He would have been clearer if he had said, not "we cannot carry our inferences on *in infinitum*" but "we cannot trace them back *in infinitum*". But as we have said, cause and effect are taken by him to be inferentially symmetrical. So for him the tracing back is inference too. But note that it must be purely *hypothetical* inference.

Let us see what this looks like in the case in hand.

Let

p = Caesar was killed

q = There were [at least ostensible] eyewitnesses of Caesar's killing

r = There was testimony from the eyewitnesses

s = There were records made, deriving from the testimony

t = There are characters and letters to be seen which say that Caesar was killed.

We must suppose that we start (how? – but let that not delay us) with the mere idea of Caesar's death. Perhaps we really do infer an effect from it as cause: "There will have been chaos and panic in the Senate when Caesar was killed." But "we must establish the existence of this cause". As we have seen, this will not be as (at the beginning) Hume suggests, by deriving it as an effect from a cause; we shall rather have to derive it as a cause from an effect. So we reason – and here our reasoning must be "purely suppositious and hypothetical" –: if p, then q; if q, then r, then s; if s, then t. Not all these hypothetical propositions are equally convincing, but only this is a chain of inferences through causes and effects such as Hume envisages. It terminates in something that we perceive. That is the last consequent. We can assert this consequent. Now we go in the other direction: since t, s; since s, r; and so on back to p.

So Hume's thesis falls into four parts. First, a chain of reasons for a belief must terminate in something that is believed without being founded on anything else. Second, the ultimate belief must be of a quite different character from the derived beliefs: it must be perceptual belief, belief in something perceived, or presently remembered. Third, the immediate justification for a belief p, if the belief is not a perception, will be another belief q, which follows from, just as much as it implies, p. Fourth, we believe by inference through the links in a chain of record.

There is an implicit corollary: when we believe in historical information belonging to the remote past, we believe that there has been a chain of record.

Hume must believe all this: otherwise he could not, however confusedly, cite the chain of record back to the eyewitnesses as an illustration of the chain of inferences *via* cause and effect, with which we cannot run up *in infinitum*.

But it is not like that. *If* the written records that we now see are grounds of our belief, they are first and foremost grounds for belief in Caesar's killing, belief that the assassination is a solid bit of history. Then our belief in that original event is a ground for belief in much of the intermediate transmission.

For let us ask: why do we believe that there were eyewitnesses of that killing? Certainly for no other reason than that we believe it happened. We infer q from p, not p from q. I have heard that the Rabbis held that the 600,000 witnesses to the crossing of the Red Sea must be credited.[2] 600,000 witnesses! That's a lot. But now: why does anyone believe there were 600,000 witnesses? – Because he believes that 600,000 passed through. And let us make no mistake: it is not otherwise for belief in there having been eyewitnesses to Caesar's assassination.

Compare one's belief in the spatio-temporal continuity of the existence of

---

[2] I owe this information to Dr Stephen Katz.

a man whom one recognizes and identifies as a man seen last week. We don't believe in the identity because we believe in the spatio-temporal continuity of a human pattern from now here to then there. It is the other way about – On the other hand a proof of a *break* in the continuity – a proof that this man was in New York in between, while that man was not – would destroy our belief in the identity. *Mutatis mutandis* the same holds for the chain of transmission of historical information.

It is so also with proper names. In using proper names that we take to be the names of people we don't know, or people in the remote past, we implicitly depend on an 'apostolical succession' of users of these names – or linguistic transforms of them – going back to original users, who knew the people. We do not, and usually could not, *trace* the chain of use of the name. But a discovery that a name belonged originally to a period later than the life-time of the supposed bearer of the name at any rate reduces the status of the name: it becomes equivalent to some set of definite descriptions.

Belief in recorded history is on the whole a belief *that there has been* a chain of tradition of reports and records going back to contemporary knowledge; it is not a belief in the historical facts by an inference that passes through the links of such a chain. At most, that can very seldom be the case.

II

All this is not just catching Hume out in a mistake. That would not be very interesting or important. The mistake – which I think it is now not a bit of patronizing superiority *more hodierno* to refer to as such – has the rare character of being easily demonstrated while yet it touches the nerve of a problem of some depth. It is a lot more difficult to see what to say, than it is to point clearly to error in Hume.

One of the rare pieces of stupidity in the writings of Wittgenstein concerns this matter:

> That it is thinkable that we may yet find Caesar's body hangs directly together with the sense of a proposition about Caesar. But so too does the possibility of finding something written, from which it emerges that no such man ever lived, and his existence was made up for particular ends. (*Philosophische Bemerkungen*, IV, 56)

What document or inscription could be evidence that Julius Caesar never existed? What would we *think* for example of an inscription saying "I, Augustus Caesar, invented the story of the divine Julius so that Caesars should be worshipped; but he never existed"? To ask a question Wittgenstein asked much later: what would get judged by what here?[3]

Take something a bit less extreme: a document recounting a conversation about siege-engines between Caesar and Archimedes. We will suppose that the document itself gets acknowledged by experts in such matters as a

---

[3] In *On Certainty*. When he wrote *On Certainty* Wittgenstein would not have made such a suggestion. I am a good deal indebted to *On Certainty* in this article.

genuine old MS. Dispute exists, perhaps, whether it was made in the tenth or eleventh century and it comes under much critical scrutiny. (It is no Piltdown skull.) The Hellenicity or Latinity is authentically ancient; it seems reasonable to place the writing of it in the first century BC. The style is such as might fit, if possible, with its being a piece of historical writing. (Xenophon's *Cyropaedeia*[4] is an example of such writing.) The content proves it to be fictitious.

It might well be that the discovery of such a piece would compel some adjustment in our picture of what was 'on' in the literature of the time. It could not force an adjustment in our idea of the relative dates of Archimedes and Caesar.

Of course Wittgenstein doesn't tell us from what character of document that could 'emerge'. I do not believe he could.

If you go to an expert on Julius Caesar, you will find he is an expert on whether Caesar conducted such and such negotiations with Pompey or when he wrote his books, for example. Not on whether Caesar existed. Contrast an expert on King Arthur.

I was taught, I think, that when Lucretius was first published during the Renaissance, the *De Rerum Natura* was suspected of being a forgery; but its Latinity and the absence of 'giveaways' won its acceptance. That means that there were standards by which to judge. The ancient Latinity of Horace, Ovid, Virgil, Cicero and Caesar was such a standard, itself known by tradition and never subject to question. The attempt to construct a serious doubt whether we have writings of Cicero – how could it find a ground from which to proceed?

We know about Caesar from the testimony of ancient historians, we even have his own writings! And how do you know *that* those are ancient historians, and these, works of Caesar? You were told it. And how did your teachers know? They were told it.

We know it from being taught; not just from explicit teaching, but by its being implicit in a lot else that we are taught explicitly. But it is very difficult to characterize the peculiar solidity involved, or its limits. It wasn't an accident that Hume took the killing of Caesar as his example; he was taking something which existed in his culture, and exists in ours, with a particular logical status of one *kind* of certainty. And yet he got a detail wrong! And yet again, that detail's being right would not be an important aspect of what he knew. I mean, if he had been careful, he could have called that in question; he could even perhaps have called the date in question (*might* it not have been a false accretion?) – but that that man, Caesar, existed and that his life terminated in assassination: this he could call in question only by indulging in Cartesian doubt.

I cannot check that there was such a person as Julius Caesar. No one can except by finding out the status of the information about him. I mean: suppose there were a schoolchild who first ran into Caesar through

[4] Thought to be history in a time of very sketchy impressions of ancient Persian history.

Shakespeare's play. Somehow he doesn't learn at once that this is not a purely fictitious story. He refers to Caesar as a fictitious character, and then someone tells him Caesar was a real historical character. *He* can check this; he can look into history books and find out that that's what Caesar is. But I cannot. I already know – I can at best remind myself of – the status of "Julius Caesar" as a name of an immensely famous man 'in history'. (To be sure, these things can change.)

Or again: suppose a Chinese man, of a time when there was little contact, who hears of Caesar from a traveller. He is accustomed to chronicles and traditional information. (But we should not forget that it is by traditional, oral, information that one knows that these *are* chronicles, or *are* editions of ancient books.) He learns that Caesar is supposed to be such a character in our history. He *can* check on it. He can learn our languages, come to our countries, find out that the corpus of solid historical information belonging to our culture does indeed include this. But I cannot. The most I can do is: frame the hypothesis that Caesar never existed, or was not assassinated, and see that it is incapable of status even as a wild hypothesis. So I do not mean that it is vastly improbable. I mean that either I should start to say: "How could one explain all these references and implications, then? . . . but, but, *but* if I doubt the existence of Caesar, if I say I may reasonably call it in question, then with equal reason I must doubt the status of the things I've just pointed to" – *or* I should realize straight away that the 'doubt' put me in a vacuum in which I could not produce reasons why such and such 'historical facts' are more or less doubtful.

I once asked an expert on Galen how he knew that his subject existed. His reaction was to consider the hypothesis that Galen did not exist. "It wouldn't do, you know," he said; "we know too much about him –" and went on to mention Galen's connection with Marcus Aurelius as an example. The response was surely a correct one. *What* does the hypothesis amount to in face of our information about the time? But if all that is irrelevant – as we could have no reason for doubting the existence of Caesar, say, but continuing to believe in Cicero and Pompey – then the effect of the hypothesis is to make a vacuum in which there is nothing by which to judge anything else.

The hypothesis about Galen is merely one that 'won't do'! That is: one can relate him to better known historical matters. But in face of such an hypothesis about Caesar one would have to ask: "What am I allowed to count as evidence, then?"

People 'in history', as we say, are not in any case hypotheses which we have arrived at to explain certain phenomena. No more than is the fact of my birth or the existence of my great-grandmothers . . . Though I have never given the question any thought before this, I know I had more than one. Do I know I had four? I would have said so. But not in the sense that the hypothesis that one of my grandfathers was a half brother, say, of the other is such that the supposition of its truth involves destroying bases and standards for discovering any historical facts at all. – And so also about people 'in history' there are gradations; and there is the possibility of discovering that some obscure supposed historical figure is probably mythical, or is a conflation or the like. Things get corrected or amended because of inconsistencies. But not everything can be put up for checking. Neurath's image is of a ship which we repair – and, I suppose, build on to – while it is afloat: if this suggests that we can go round tapping every plank for rottenness, and so we might end up with a wholly different ship, the analogy is not good. For there are things that are on a level. A general epistemological reason for doubting one will be a reason for doubting all, and then none of them would have anything to test it by.

10 "Whatever has a Beginning of Existence must have a Cause"

Hume's Argument Exposed

In *A Treatise of Human Nature*, Book I, Part III, Section II, Hume distinguishes two questions, the one: *Why a beginning of existence must necessarily always have a cause?* and the other, a double one: *Why we conclude that such particular causes must necessarily have such particular effects; and what is the nature of the inference, from the one to the other?*

Not only are these distinct questions but a person may consistently hold that a beginning of existence must always have a cause, without holding that "such particular causes must have such particular effects" (or that such particular effects must have such particular causes). It isn't clear whether Hume saw this.

His most famous thesis is that the ideas of cause and effect are always separable; that is, that one may, without contradiction or absurdity, suppose a given sort of cause to occur without its characteristic effect, and vice versa. This *seems* to be very generally true. There is a counter-example. If I ask how something comes to be in a certain place, I may learn that it arrived there from somewhere else; i.e. it travelled from point A to point B from time t to t' and so was at point B at t'. This is a causal explanation of its coming to be at point B at t' and it cannot "without contradiction or absurdity" be supposed to happen without the thing's coming to be at point B – an event that might, however, have occurred otherwise, if for example it came into existence at that moment at that place. Thus, we can't accept Hume's principle as impregnable. But it is *prima facie* true in a vast number of cases.

Section III of Part III, Book I of the *Treatise* is devoted to proving that "Whatever begins to exist must have a cause of existence" is not intuitively or demonstrably certain, i.e. is not what would nowadays be called a proposition whose truth is logically necessary.

What Hume calls "intuitively certain" is a proposition whose truth is discoverable purely from examining the ideas contained in it, and what he calls "demonstrably certain" is apparently a proposition which follows from something intuitively certain.

He first produces a 'proof', which we shall soon examine, that that first 'principle of causality' cannot possibly be intuitively or demonstrably certain; and he devotes the rest of the section to disposing of such arguments

From *Analysis*, 34, 5 (1974).

as he knows, purporting to demonstrate it. He considers four arguments, of which he is able to refute the last three quite easily; indeed they do not deserve attention. One says that something that came into existence without a cause must produce itself, which is impossible; another, that it is produced by *nothing*, which is incapable of producing anything. As Hume says, these arguments assume what they set out to prove, and so can hardly prove it. This is not "just reasoning". The point is obvious indeed. Not that the arguments are invalid; but they cannot prove the conclusion, if they cannot prove it except to someone who already accepts it. Another argument Hume reasonably calls still more frivolous: every effect must have a cause, since cause and effect are relative terms. As he says, this does not show that every beginning of existence must be an effect, any more than the truth that every husband must have a wife shows that every man must be married. His making this point will be of some importance for our understanding of his positive argument that this 'principle of causality' cannot possibly be intuitively or demonstrably certain. So much for the second, third and fourth arguments which he considers.

The first argument, however, is obscure and is dealt with rather sketchily. It is that "all the points of time and space, in which we can suppose any object to begin to exist, are in themselves equal; and unless there be some cause, which is peculiar to one time and to one place, and which by that means determines and fixes the existence, it must remain in eternal suspense". Hume replies:

> Is there any more difficulty in supposing the time and place to be fix'd without a cause, than to suppose the existence to be determin'd in that manner? The first question that occurs on this subject is always, *whether* the object shall exist or not: the next, *when* and *where* it shall begin to exist. If the removal of a cause be intuitively absurd in the one case, it must be so in the other: and if that absurdity be not clear without a proof in the one case, it will equally require one in the other. The absurdity, then, of the one supposition can never be a proof of that of the other, since they are both upon the same footing, and must stand or fall by the same reasoning.

Why does he say "The first question is whether an object shall exist"? This seems to consider the matter from the point of view of a creator, which suggests that Hume is consciously in Leibniz country; for Leibniz argues for the identity of indiscernibles on the ground that God must have a reason for putting A here and now, and B there and then, which there could not be unless something distinguished A from B. Yet Hume doesn't consider this. The questions are not easy to reformulate and seem better left out.

What is Hume's argument? He is saying: You cannot argue to the absurdity of p, from the fact that it entails q, which is absurd, for if someone saw no difficulty in p, he'd see no difficulty in q. (Rather as if the argument were a shaggy dog story.) This is somewhat cavalier. The arguer is not saying "There is no absurdity in p but there is in q", but rather "There is at any rate *this* absurdity in p, that it entails q, which is absurd".

Hume is saying "But why should I find q absurb, if I don't *already* find p absurd?" And to this there may well be an answer in this case. It is not fair to say: you *cannot* argue like that, because you are initially supposing that p is *not* absurd. One is not initially supposing anything of the sort. Well, Hume says, by producing an argument instead of simply saying p is absurd, you are conceding it is not intuitively absurd; now *if* it is not intuitively absurd, then neither is q. Well, even that is not clear, but anyway, perhaps q is not 'intuitively' absurd but there are further arguments to show that q is absurd.

And this is indeed the case. Without existing at a definite place and time, a particular finite and non-eternal thing won't exist at all. Hobbes' argument, as cited by Hume, seems to go on as follows: Antecedently to a thing's existence at a place and time nothing can connect it with that time and place more than with any other, unless something already existent makes that the time and place of the thing's existence. This argument indeed seems very uncertain. Hume could say: the thing is and can be connected with the time and place *only* by the brute fact of existing then and there: you can think of that without invoking something else that makes it exist at that time and place.

But the argument suggests another one. Namely: space and time are relative, that is, antecedently to a thing's existence at a place and time, there can be no distinction of that place and time from any other unless something else distinguishes them. In this passage, Hume writes as if the place and time for a thing's existence could be specified independently of its existence. The argument that he is considering assumes that too; and also it is the truth. Since, then, space and time are relative, this specifiability requires a determinant other than the thing which is supposed to exist, or to have existed, in the place and at the time.

That is the argument, and Hume does not deal with the questions suggested by the argument he cited from Hobbes, which give rise to this one: he has apparently not seen that the question arises what the requisite specification of place and time could mean without a prior existence. Or at least *some* other existence. For as far as concerns time, it may not be prior; it might be posterior. Thus we specify a time as n years ago. This is not to give a cause, but the requirement of other existences by which to specify time and place does disprove Hume's great principle "That there is nothing in any object consider'd in itself, which can afford us a reason for drawing a conclusion beyond it" (Selby-Bigge's edition, p. 139). Or if he should say: "consider'd in itself" excludes "consider'd as existing at a given time and place", then, if a thing that comes into existence must come into existence at a given time and place, 'consider'd in itself' it can't be considered as coming into existence at all. But as soon as you consider it as existing at a given time and place, the question arises as to how that time and place could be specified.

This is a very obscure topic, and we will leave it, with the observation that Hume has hardly done it justice. Let us now attend to our main business: the argument, already given by him, to show that a beginning of existence without a cause is not demonstrably absurd.

It is an argument from imagination.

As all distinct ideas are separable from each other, and as the ideas of cause and effect are evidently distinct, 'twill be easy for us to conceive any object to be non-existent this moment, and existent the next, without conjoining to it the distinct idea of a cause or productive principle. The separation, therefore, of the idea of a cause from that of a beginning of existence is plainly possible for the imagination, and consequently the actual separation of these objects is so far possible, that it implies no contradiction or absurdity. (pp. 79–80)

His argument is rather prolix – more so than my quotation shows. Let us set it out proposition by proposition.

(1) All distinct ideas are separable.
(2) The ideas of cause and effect are distinct.
(3) ∴ It will be easy to think of an object's coming into existence without thinking of a cause.

So far, so good: "separable" presumably means "such that one can think of one without *eo ipso* thinking of the other".

We might query (2) on the grounds that cause and effect are correlative, like husband and wife. But from Hume's giving an example of an effect in (3), and especially in view of his calling "frivolous" the argument that the ideas of cause and effect are correlative, we must take him to mean that the ideas of whatever objects are causes and effects are distinct from one another. The next step is the crucial one:

(4) ∴ The separation of the idea of a cause from that of a beginning of existence is possible for the imagination.

What does this mean? There are two possibilities: that it is possible to imagine a beginning of existence without imagining a cause, and that it is possible to imagin ne a beginning of existence without a cause. The first certainly follows from (3) but is too close to it in sense for us seriously to suppose it is what Hume means. He must, then, mean the second, so we have

(4a) ∴ It is possible to imagine something's beginning to exist without a cause.

From this he draws the conclusion

(5) ∴ The actual separation of these objects is so far possible, that it implies no contradiction or absurdity.

This makes one ask "What objects?" The answer, as far as concerns one of them, is plain: it is "a beginning of existence".

For example, I imagine a star or a rabbit beginning to exist. To supply such a particular case is both reasonable and conformable to Hume's doctrine of abstract ideas; for neither in reality nor according to Hume can there be a bare image of a beginning of existence which is not the beginning of existence of anything in particular. But what is the other 'object'? The only answer we have is "a cause". Now we can go two ways. We can either forsake the doctrine of abstract ideas and say that that is to be a sufficient description of our image in the particular case, or we can, as we did with "a beginning of existence", supply a specific cause, as, another rabbit, or the compacting of nebulous material. And here arises the difficulty. For the argument from imaginability to possibility has a good deal of force on the second interpretation: let me imagine any event – say the boiling of a kettle – and any particular cause of it – say the heat of a fire, and not only can I imagine the one's happening without the other, but the imaginability is of a sort to convince me of the possibility in the sense of 'implying no contradiction or absurdity'. "I know what it would be like to find a kettle boiled without a fire," I may say, and even "I know what it would be like to find a rabbit coming into being *not* from a parent rabbit". So here the argument from imagination is sound. But this sound argument does not yield the desired conclusion. Let it hold for any particular cause I care to introduce. Let us even suppose that Hume is right in saying it holds universally. Then I can say

(6) For any beginning (or modification) of existence E and any particular cause C, I can imagine E's happening without C,

and infer from this

(7) For any beginning (or modification) of existence E, and any particular cause C, E can be supposed to happen without C: i.e. there is no contradiction or absurdity in the supposition.

But the proposition does not give me the possibility of imagining an effect without any cause at all. That is, it does not give me:

(8) I can imagine this: there is a beginning (or modification) of existence without any cause.

For quite generally from

For *any*, it is possible that not . . .

there does not follow:

It is possible that for *none* . . .

For example, from:

For *any* colour, I can imagine that a rose is not that colour

does not follow:

I can imagine that a rose has no colour.

Nor does, (6), the possible exclusion of any particular cause in the imagination, or what (we are granting) follows from it, (7), the possibility of a beginning of existence without any given cause, yield

(9) A beginning of existence can *happen* without any cause,

i.e. this supposition is without contradiction or absurdity.

So if we go this way we have (perhaps) a sound argument from imagination. "This can be imagined, therefore this is possible," but the *this* is not the desired conclusion, but is only the conclusion that the effect can occur without any particular cause which you have imagined it without.

We must, then, try the other tack, in which we forget Hume's doctrine of abstract ideas, and accept that the second 'object' is just 'a cause' and no more. Then the argument is simply:

> We can imagine something's coming into existence without a cause.
> ∴ It is possible (i.e. there is no contradiction in supposing) that something comes into existence without a cause.

If this is the right interpretation, one wonders why Hume did not give the argument straight in this form. The trouble about it is that it is very unconvincing. For if I say I can imagine a rabbit coming into being without a parent rabbit, well and good: I imagine a rabbit coming into being, and our observing that there is no parent rabbit about. But what am I to imagine if I imagine a rabbit coming into being without a cause? Well, I just imagine a rabbit appearing. That this *is* the imagination of a rabbit coming into being, and without a cause is nothing but, as it were, the *title* of the picture. Indeed I can form an image and give my picture that title. But from my being able to do *that*, nothing whatever follows about what is possible to suppose "without contradiction or absurdity" as holding in reality.

Hume's argument can be rendered more intelligible to us if we attribute to him the following principle:

> If a circumstance need not be thought of in thinking of a thing, then that thing can be thought of as lacking that circumstance and hence can exist without it.

The attribution is probably correct; for we know that Hume thought that *"the mind cannot form any notion of quantity or quality without forming a precise notion of degrees of each"* (p. 18). His argument for this is that, e.g., the 'precise degree of any quality' cannot be distinguished from the quality. Holding it obviously absurd to suppose a quality to exist, though in no particular degree, Hume thought there could be no such thing as an idea of it which was not an idea of any particular degree of it. Generalizing, we may put it:

> If something cannot be without such and such, it cannot be thought of without thinking of such and such.

The principle we have attributed to Hume as inspiring the argument we have been examining is essentially this one contraposed, though an extra step has been put in.

With some caution and restriction, we may grant the Parmenidean principle that "It is the same thing that can be thought and can be". But Hume's extension of it is certainly wrong. It is even wrong in the particular case from which we formed the generalization. I can imagine or think of a sprig of leaves as existing without there being any definite number of leaves that I think of it as having. Naturally, this does not mean that I can think of it as existing without having a definite number of leaves.

11 Will and Emotion

Brentano's *Psychologie vom empirischen Standpunkt* is a work which belies its title. It would perhaps be correct if *"empirischen"* had been altered to *"empiristischen"*. – It labours on the one hand to *separate* imagination and judgement into two fundamental distinct classes of psychological phenomena, and on the other to *associate* will and emotion or even to identify an act of will as the occurrence of an emotion, though Brentano will grant that people will hardly *call* it emotion. The former enterprise is vitiated by his failure to distinguish between predication and assertion. He says of the copula that it ". . . nur den Ausdruck von Vorstellungen zum Ausdrucke eines anerkennenden oder verwerfenden Urteils ergänze. . . ." (Bd. 2, Kap, 7) However, this was an almost universal error; it took Frege to distinguish predication from assertion, and Brentano is surely right in combating the Humean thesis that there is no difference between mere images, and, say, propositions or their content. Brentano's second enterprise is to my mind the more interesting and powerful. He puts the act of will (in a particular case) at one end of a spectrum of emotions:

> Betrachten wir als Beispiel die folgende Reihe: Traurigkeit – Sehnsucht nach dem vermißten Gute – Hoffnung, daß es uns zuteil werde – Verlangen, es uns zu verschaffen – Mut, den Versuch zu unternehmen – Willensentschluß zur Tat. Das eine Extrem ist ein Gefühl, das andere ein Willen; und sie scheinen weit voneinander abzustehen. Wenn man aber auf die Zwischenglieder achtet und immer nur die nächststehenden miteinander vergleicht, zeigt sich da nicht überall der innigste Anschluß und ein fast unmerklicher Übergang? (Bd. 2, Kap. 8)

The list doesn't include fear, but might easily have done so: it could go in after longing. Now, he says, isn't the act of will which he puts in as the last member of the series, and which comes after 'Mut', that is, *spirit* to make the attempt – isn't it *extremely* like that spirit, that sentiment of boldness or courage, that *nerving* of oneself, as we say? In illustration, imagine a young person standing outside the door of someone alarming, whom he is summoning up the courage to beard. He has just nerved himself to walk in, he has arrived at the state of 'Mut'. Now consider the *next* thing, before he actually pushes the door open and steps forward. If we *can* insert something psychological, something inner, in there at all – something which belongs in the *development* which is to culminate in action, won't it be *almost* the same as the 'Mut' itself, only *more committed* to the action? To see that we might do so, consider that he might summon up the 'Mut' and then realize that the action was impossible – he perceives that the swing door is locked. He physically can't push it open. Now if that's what happens, he hasn't even tried to do it.

In just the same situation, in which however he doesn't notice the metal tongue of the lock in position, given that little extra, the act of will itself, he won't indeed push the door open (for he can't) but he will have tried. So there is a difference between this last term and the 'Mut', but how small! And aren't they obviously the same in kind? If there *is* that last term there at all, it clearly belongs to the same class as the 'Mut', and hence in the same class as all the rest. And so we have will assimilated to emotion. This is developed into the characterization of emotions (and therefore will) as a set of states or events whose common theme is acceptability or unacceptability, not as true or false but in another way, of possible contents of judgement. These states or events are differentiated from one another by the peculiar colouring associated with each.

Note that we are persuaded to make the assimilation by a rather special type of example. Where no 'Mut' is needed one couldn't find a likeness, even if one assumed an intercalated act of will, when one was describing some act like picking up a glass of milk to drink it.

Brentano however is pointing to *some* conceptual relationship – in him it is an assimilation – between will and the emotions. Nor is he alone in this. Augustine makes a certain assimilation too:

> Voluntas est quippe in omnibus: immo omnes nihil aliud quam voluntates sunt. Nam quid est cupiditas et laetitia, nisi voluntas in eorum consensione, quae volumus? et quid est metus et tristitia, nisi voluntas in dissensione ab his, quae nolumus? Sed cum consentimus appetendo ea quae volumus, cupiditas; cum autem consentimus fruendo his quae volumus, laetitia vocatur. Itemque cum dissentimus ab eo quod accidere nolumus, talis voluntas metus est; cum autem dissentimus ab eo quod nolentibus accidit, talis voluntas tristitia est. (*De Civitate Dei* Lib. XIV, Cap. VI)

"There is will in all of them," he says, "Nay, they are nothing but wills." You may think this isn't like Brentano, who is talking about a will that occurs just prior to an act: Augustine *calls* the principal passions all will and Brentano would *like* to call will *a* passion, one member of that class. But look a little more closely. The contrast isn't so great. Augustine is concerned with just four generic emotions, fear and desire, distress and joy. "For what are desire and joy but will, saying yes [consenting] to the things we want? And what are fear and sorrow but will, saying no to [dissenting from] the things we don't want? When we consent, seeking what we want, that's desire, but when we consent, having the things we want, that is called joy." And likewise, he goes on, (*mutatis mutandis*) for fear and distress.

We find Augustine's 'yes' and 'no' in Brentano too:

> Wenn etwas Inhalt eines Urteils werden kann, insofern es als wahr annehmlich oder als falsch verwerflich ist, so kann es Inhalt eines Phänomens der dritten Grundklasse werden, insofern es als gut genehm (im weitesten Sinne des Wortes) oder als schlecht ungenehm sein kann.

The comparison had already been made in respect of desire, *orexis*, in a very generic sense of the term, by Aristotle:

ἐστι δ' ὅπερ ἐν διανοίᾳ κατάφασις καὶ ἀπόφασις, τουτ' ἐν ὀρέξει δίωξις καὶ φυγή
(What ascription and denial are in judgement, pursuit and avoidance are in desire.)
(*Nicomachean Ethics*, 1139a, 21–2)

Aristotle's *orexis* covers sensual desire (*epithumia*) and anger (*thumos*) as well as wish, decision and choice. In the passage I quote some might claim that he doesn't mean to refer to the passions, because the passage is leading up to the explanation of choice. But since the passions are certainly causes of pursuit and avoidance this doesn't seem sound. So we can after all put him with Augustine and Brentano here. *All* of them speak of, or make a comparison with yes and no when they consider will and desire.

As soon as you make this comparison you are faced with the equivalence of "no", in response to a negative, and "yes" in response to the corresponding positive. Does this carry through to emotion and will? Here we can ask various questions:

(1) Is pleasure ('Lust') at the idea of something's occurring equivalent to, or does it necessarily involve pain, distress ('Unlust') at the idea of its *not* occurring? To this the answer seems to be clear, that there is no such connection.

(2) If you are willing that something should happen, must you be unwilling that it should not happen? Obviously not.

(3) If you want something to happen, must you want it not to fail to happen? Here the answer is positive. Though, by the way, this doesn't mean that wants must be consistent – nothing is said about whether you can *also* want it to fail to happen. Similarly when we say that one who believes p disbelieves not p we haven't said yet whether he can *also* believe not p.

(4) If you hope that something will happen, must you fear that it will not? Here (*pace* Spinoza) the answer seems to be: not generally. But hope and fear are tied up with *expectation* in complicated ways, and there is no doubt a host of cases where hope of something does involve fear of the contrary, at least if the thought of that is entertained. Nevertheless, one character may be fearful more than hopeful, and another the opposite.

Belief equals disbelief in the contradictory and any proposition can be given a negative form. Therefore to say that someone is characterized by believingness rather than disbelievingness is to say nothing. Unless it means that he tends – more strongly than most people – to believe what he is told rather than to disbelieve it.

But does it mean nothing to say someone's belief attitudes are positive rather than negative? Well, it seems to mean something in the following way: someone may be little interested in what is not the case, and only interested in what is the case. But didn't we say that *anything* can be given a negative form? It makes no sense to say that someone is interested by the fact that some man is alive and not by the fact that he is not dead. Thus we might make a classification of certain pairs of contraries as ones which exhaust the possibilities for their subjects, when they exist and are capable of having the predicates hold of them, e.g. 'blind', 'sighted'.

It does make sense to say of someone "He's interested in what colour something *is*, not in what colours it is *not*". And it might be complained against me, if I say what 'will' is not, but not what it is. Thus it does make sense to speak of a man's opinions, of his belief, as tending in the positive direction: he says what exists, what qualities things have, what they are, rather than what doesn't exist, what qualities things don't have, and what they aren't. Geach has written against the idea of there being any sense in positiveness of belief – with which he wants to contrast will – but he has, I think, not noticed this aspect. Belief is as its objects are. We may accept the idea of certain objects of belief as positive (whether or not their expression contains a negation) though we need have no general theory of *all* propositions as ultimately positive or negative in sense. Aristotle's theory of the categories is a theory of things which are positive in our present sense. (It is certainly not a theory of all predicates.)

This is the only way in which it makes sense to speak of belief as positive: 'positive' belief must mean belief in positive things. In this way belief that someone was dead could be called negative, belief that he was alive positive. And it might be a characteristic of someone always to relish believing negative things. But disbelief would not as such be negative, only disbelief in something positive.

Turning back to will and emotion, the idea of positive attitudes, as Geach says, is readily acceptable. Love, pleasure, joy, cheer, curiosity, hope, friendliness, surprise, admiration, gladness on anyone's behalf, 'nerve' – all these anyone will call positive. Whereas hatred, distress, sadness, gloom, depression, lack of interest, hopelessness, dislike and spite, contempt, scorn, envy (in the sense of disliking another's gain or good), fearfulness – all these will readily be counted 'negative'.

But perhaps this is no more than a 'taking as' which comes naturally to everyone? Hatred, one may say, seems a pretty positive thing when considered in itself, but when offered the choice: how will you distribute the terms "positive" and "negative" between hatred and love, then one will retreat and call hatred the negative emotion. Why? Mephistopheles says in *Faust*: "Ich bin der Geist der stets verneint" – but how does that fit with our observation that affirmation and denial of the contradictory are equivalent? If that spirit will keep a promise to say "no" to *everything*, we can get what concessions we like out of him, like the young man in the English song "O no John no John no John, No!" Goethe's line is very evocative: is it more? – Once again, the answer is yes, if we think of that spirit as the spirit of destruction of positive things. And that is the reason for the 'negativeness' of hate. Love and hate take personal objects; hating a person, one wishes that he may be destroyed or diminished. And so the 'Geist der stets verneint' thinks that 'alles was entsteht ist wert daß es zu Grunde geht' – everything that comes into being deserves to be abolished. The roots of a real polar opposition of emotions are surely to be sought here.

So long as you stick to *propositions in general* (or other possible objects of judgement) as giving the objects of emotion and will, you may indeed say that there is yes and no in them; you may compare pursuit and avoidance to affirmation and negation; but you are going to get pursuit and avoidance as equivalent to one another according as the same matter is itself presented negatively or positively. You aren't going to get any real contrast of positive and negative, or pursuit and avoidance, and it is useless to look *here* for the explanation of negativeness in will and emotion.

Yet it is precisely *here* that there is a logical similarity between will and emotion. Even emotion such as love, which doesn't 'take' propositional objects, involves desires which do. And the logical similarity is in the language connected with e.g. desire on the one hand and will on the other. In this resides the sum of correctness in Brentano's assimilation of the two kinds of thing, emotion and will.

Now I am in opposition to Brentano in respect of his assimilation. I would quite radically distinguish will and emotion and I say that Brentano assimilated them because he didn't realize *how* unlike they are. I'd want to distinguish soap from washing. – At least, the need to do so would never arise; but if anyone did assimilate soap and washing I'd want to oppose it.

In spite of this, I need not deny *one* similarity at all – I mean the similarity in language. One regrets, finds bad *that* someone is ill, one wills, takes steps, to bring it about that he *not* be ill. I don't deny this similarity, rather I energetically draw attention to it. For it's a necessary and useful point for helping to distinguish between emotions and complex bodily sensations such as dizziness, nausea, thirst, itches, weariness, sleepiness, being on edge, feeling inert, feeling full. One doesn't want to call these "emotion". But why not? The answer is that these sensations don't involve reference to good and evil, that admixture of reasons and thoughts which is so characteristic of human emotion. Nausea, for example, is a feeling of *being liable to throw up soon*, it is not a feeling that it would be good or lovely to throw up. Nor even is thirst a feeling that it would be lovely to drink – even though one might give expression to it by saying so and thereby become emotional about it. This point is by itself enough to show Brentano radically wrong in his explanation of the ideas of good and evil. (If I have understood him.) If we have to use them to differentiate emotions from psycho-somatic sensations, then they cannot be explained to us by pointing to the emotions. The genetic explanation by reference to familiar objects of experience: "You know what fear and hope, love and hate are, don't you? Well, the ideas that can be got from having all of these in your repertoire are the ideas of good and evil" – this won't work because we will already have to mention good and evil in explaining what we meant by the words for the emotions.

Brentano knows quite well that will is not a feeling: "daß er einen Willensentschluß fühle wird wohl keiner sagen." It is a point that somewhat embarrasses him, I think, and that he forgets from time to time, as when he says that inner experience shows that there is nowhere a sharp boundary between feeling and will. That suggests that he sees or wants to see an act of will as itself a content of consciousness and thinks that feeling merges into it. Indeed that was rather suggested by his spectrum. And he speaks of a "seed" of striving as already there in the feeling of yearning, of this "seed" as "sprouting" in hope, "unfolding" in wishing and in getting one's courage up, and "ripening" in the decision of the will:

Aber liegt nicht demungeachtet schon in der Sehnsucht ein Keim des Strebens? und sprießt dieser nicht auf in der Hoffnung, und entfaltet sich, bei dem Gedanken an ein etwaiges eigenes Zutun, in dem Wunsche zu handeln und in dem Mute dazu; bis endlich das Verlangen danach zugleich die Scheu vor jedem Opfer und den Wunsch jeder längeren Erwägung überwiegt und so zum Willensentschuß gereift ist?

Once again, we seem to have our attention directed to a very special sort of example. Not to such ordinary examples as the following ones: I feel inclined to shut the window and I do shut it; I have made up my mind to catch a certain train and I leave in time (or not quite in time). The idea of neighbouring members of a series which can hardly be distinguished from one another seems quite inappropriate to these cases.

That an act is voluntary doesn't mean that it is preceded by an act of will, but that it is *itself* an act of will. In proof of this, consider how, whatever inner event precedes an act, one can still ask *if it was voluntary when it occurred*. Crouching down on the edge of the swimming bath I had *just* nerved myself (Brentano's 'Mut') and positively determined to roll head first into the water – suddenly you pushed me. The physical event was almost the same. What matter that I find the *nerving myself* and the *decision* extremely alike? Neither of them was the will in the voluntary act of rolling into the water – for *ex hypothesi* there wasn't any such voluntary act.

Neither of them would have been the will *in* the voluntary act if the act *had* been voluntary. The voluntariness of the voluntary act doesn't consist in anything of the sort. Brentano, who assumes it does, *finds* something introspectively almost indistinguishable from something else, something in the line of feelings (the 'Mut') which he also finds present. But the whole idea is an error, a confusion of radically different kinds of thing, of elements in a flow of feelings with the voluntariness of an act. It is in fact as odd as identifying hunger with the voluntariness of eating, or putting them in the same class.

There is another reason for the error of psychological confusion here. We all know it is difficult to find the event which shall be the act of will within a voluntary action. But it is equally difficult to find the event which is the feeling, the emotion, once we examine the situation in detail. "I'd just nerved myself," we say: but what *was* that? A certain tension of the muscles, drawing in of the breath, a thought? "I was very angry," or "very frightened". What was that? Was there a feeling of anger or fright which occurred at a particular time? Well, yes, if you mean that at some particular time it was true that I was angry (frightened). But what was the feeling of anger or fright itself? One may find certain physical sensations – but they can't *be* the anger or fright, for one can ask someone "How does (or did) anger (or fear) take you? Where did you feel it? In your chest? In your head? In your legs?" Now suppose someone says: With me then it was a constriction in the chest and a trembling in my knees. "How did you know *that* was a sensation of anger – or fear?" – for I have deliberately chosen what might easily be either. At this point one wants to say: The feeling of anger (or fear) *suffuses* the physical sensations and the reactions in thought and action. That is why I say that this sensation was a sensation belonging to my being angry, whereas a tickle that suddenly perhaps attacked my nose at the same time had nothing to do with it. And this metaphor of suffusion is a very powerful one. Brentano himself implicitly uses it: he keeps on speaking of the different *colouring* of the different emotions – leaving one to understand perhaps that the will has yet another colour. I don't think, however, that he noticed the elusiveness of the feelings themselves, which is quite like the elusiveness of the act of will. These things elude one when one approaches the matter with a certain expectation of what one will be able to find.

This point of similarity, however, would be no ground for an assimilation. The states of emotion, whether or not they are states of actual excitation, undoubtedly *cause* both voluntary and involuntary actions. Also the emotion is mentioned as a reason or 'motive' for some actions, as well as a cause of others. Examples: I upset the coffee – involuntarily – because I was so angry; I abandoned a proposed outing because I was angry – anger had taken away my inclination to make it; I wrote that letter because I was angry – i.e. anger inspired it. It would be of interest to discuss the causality – i.e. how many different types there are here. Lack of space prevents this. But at least the effect is of a quite different kind from the cause: the effect is a voluntary action taking place no doubt at a definite time; the cause, a state which lacks a central core and the assignment of which to a definite time, though sometimes possible, is by no means necessary. There need be no answer to the question when one began to fear something, or when one stopped; though it may be certain that one did fear it at a certain given date, and that this had certain consequences, some of which can be called effects.

It is difficult for Brentano not to turn out to be an emotivist. For he thinks the source of the ideas of good and bad is purely experiences of love and hate (taken very broadly). Thus he quotes with approval a remark of Kant's in *Untersuchungen über die Deutlichkeit der Grundsätze der natürlichen Theologie und Moral*, to the effect that only now are we at last realizing that, as knowledge (*Erkenntnis*) is the source of the power of imagining what is true, so feeling is the source of the power of experiencing what is good:

Man hat es in unseren Tagen allererst einzusehen angefangen, daß das Vermögen das Wahre vorzustellen, die Erkenntnis, dasjenige aber, das Gute zu empfinden, das Gefühl sei, und daß beide ja nicht miteinander müssen verwechselt werden.

So we see the drive behind his contention of the identity in kind between will and the emotions: it doesn't belong to the intelligence to frame the ideas of good and evil. But the contention fails, is void for uncertainty, because will is far *more* different in kind from the emotions than he ever even conceived as a position for his opponents to take up. To will is *either* (a) to make some decision – but no such thing as a distinct mental act is generally necessary when one acts voluntarily – *or* (b) to have a certain intention – as, e.g. I have an intention of returning to England this month, and have had it all along without thinking of it (otherwise than by booking the passage: certainly *that* is nothing of the same kind as a feeling) *or* (c) to *try* to do something (which is usually to do something *else*) *or* (d) to act voluntarily. The last is the important case for us – the others are side issues. A positive act of mine is voluntary, not because it is accompanied or preceded by an act of will, but because it is done by me either for its own sake or for the sake of something else. This new dimension of 'What for?' enters into the description of the act and belongs to the intelligence of the agent. It belongs to intelligence in two ways: one, that intelligence grasps what conduces to what and what the situation is in which it operates; and two, that it frames the conceptions of those generic (right or wrong) ends which are characteristic of human beings. I mean that e.g. other animals may be dominated by an appetite for pleasure; but it takes intelligence of the human sort to be an *akolastos* in Aristotle's sense and make pleasure in general one's goal.

12   Retractation

Here is a striking fact about the *Tractatus*: the question whether the *objects* spoken of there are individuals only or are also universals seems not to have crossed Wittgenstein's mind. This fact has always made me uneasy over exegetes' taking sides on this question: Erik Stenius giving one answer, and Irving Copi and myself, for example, another.[1] Professor Stenius does indeed cast some doubt on the suitability of the traditional term "universals"; but he says it is a term used for what he calls "predicates" (relations and properties). And he insists that there are these two quite different kinds of 'objects' – individuals and predicates. This leads him to a really monstrous piece of exegesis: he simply overrides Wittgenstein's statement that names resemble points in that they lack *Sinn*, reversible polarity, i.e. negatability or, in Stenius' phrase, directed meaning. Referring to the way in which predicate-expressions, unlike names, admit of negation, he says "Thus Wittgenstein is wrong when he says in 3.144 that (all) names resemble 'points'. Names of *predicates* are more like 'arrows' because their meaning is 'directed'" (p. 175).

I still think Stenius quite wrong about this; but I now think that Ramsey was righter than I ever realized.[2] Ramsey disputed the distinction between individuals and universals on the ground that there was no less reason to speak of Socrates as attaching to wisdom, say, than to speak of wisdom as attaching to Socrates. Wisdom is found in many objects; but equally Socrates has many things true of him; the one-in-many theme does not come out in only one way as between Socrates and wisdom.

What Ramsey failed to see was the distinction between the sign of a function and a name; he did not perceive that what signally distinguishes names from expressions for predicates is that expressions for predicates can be negated, names not. I mean that negation, attached to a predicate, yields a new predicate, but when attached to a name it does not yield any name. Oddly, too, he seems to have thought of "f(b)", one of the notations for an elementary proposition in the *Tractatus*, as if the possible atomic fact it would symbolize must consist of two objects, f and b. These errors can be avoided, however, while Ramsey's essential idea is kept.

Frege had distinguished concept and object; concepts, the reference of predicates, were essentially 'unsaturated'; a concept had as it were a hole in it, waiting to be filled by an object. Ramsey objected to this idea, whose

---

[1] Erik Stenius, *Wittgenstein's Tractatus* (Oxford, 1960); Irving Copi, 'Objects, Properties, and Relations in the *Tractatus*', *Mind*, 67 (1958); G. E. M. Anscombe, *An Introduction to Wittgenstein's Tractatus* (London, 1959).

[2] F. P. Ramsey, 'Universals' in *The Foundations of Mathematics* (London, 1931).

exposition he found in Russell. He said that *both* parts of the proposition –
name and predicate-expression – stood for incomplete objects and that
there was no essential difference between universals and particulars. Both
could exist only in facts, i.e. in combination.

Protesting that "f (b)" need not for Wittgenstein represent only a two-
object atomic fact, I myself came to think that there could be no such fact –
though, mysteriously, the *Tractatus* forbids one to *say* so. In Wittgenstein, I
maintained, predicates, concepts, or universals are not just more objects, as
Ramsey took it, nor yet another sort of object, as Stenius takes it; rather,
Wittgenstein made the gulf between concept and object far greater than
Frege did. So far as concerned the *meaning* of a functional expression, this
was simply objects; but in respect of having argument-places, concepts go
over entirely into logical forms; the completely analysed proposition is, as
Wittgenstein himself later put it, "a logical network sprinkled with names".
It is this logical network alone that is 'universal' and in its connection arises
the possibility of negation, logical product, logical sum, etc. This view still
appears to me to be correct; but I see no reason to insist that a functional
expression always 'covers', as I put it, more than one name. This expression
is mine, not Wittgenstein's; but I think it is justified, e.g. by that phrase "a
logical network sprinkled with names", which he later used to characterize
the *Tractatus* position.

There is an ambiguity of the word "predicate" that needs clearing up.
Predicate-expressions, I hold, are not names, and the only objects admitted
in the *Tractatus* are the bearers of names. Now if predicates are what is symbolized by the remainder of a proposition when one *or more* names are
deleted, then there will be predicates of different type – monadic, dyadic, etc.
This, however, is not the way in which "predicate" was used in early Russell.
There a 'subject-predicate proposition' was a non-relational one; a proposition in which a non-relational property was ascribed to a subject. This is
Wittgenstein's usage in 4.1274: "one cannot ask: are there unanalysable
subject-predicate propositions?" Hence he implies here that one cannot ask
whether there are possible atomic facts containing just two objects. This pro-
hibition worried me; for at that time it certainly appeared to me that one
must say there could not be; any predicate would have to cover a plurality of
names. I complained that Ramsey wrote as if, say "a–b" were a specifiable
elementary proposition, which Wittgenstein chooses to write as, say, "f(b)".
"f(b)", I said, symbolizes an elementary proposition, but not necessarily one
in whose sense *only* two objects occur. This still seems certainly right; but
there is nothing *against* a functional expression "f" covering only one name.
Thus, if an elementary proposition could be reached in a particular case, and
"a–b" were the elementary proposition fully analysed into a concatenation
of names, it could be regarded as the result of completing a function "f(x)"
by "b" as giving a value of "x", or a different function "g (x)" by "a". Here
"f" would not be another *name* of a, or "g" another *name* of b, though both
"f(b)" and "g(a)" would be equivalent to "a–b". But *logic* has nothing to say

as to whether there are or are not such elementary propositions, and ordinary language uses propositions of the subject-predicate *form* without enquiry into their analysability.

There *is* indeed the contrast, strongly insisted on in the *Tractatus*, between name and function. This contrast is disregarded by both Stenius and Ramsey; and I thought it was the same as – or simply the 'formal mode' for – the contrast between individual and universal, and so failed to take Ramsey's point. The fact that we *must* contrast name and function does not in the least oblige us to deny that the objects (whatever they are) covered by "red" in "A is red" could *also* enter into the fact that B is red. (Even if A and B are different and widely separated things.)

Denying this, I wrote of it as a purely Ramseyesque view:

> The question arises whether the objects that would be named in place of our using the colour-word "red" in the two cases, would be different. I think Ramsey would have supposed they would be the same. And no doubt he would have pooh-poohed the feeling that in that case these objects would have the character of universals rather than 'individuals': we don't think A is a universal because it can enter into a variety of facts, so why should we think this of red – or, if red is composite, of the objects into which red is analysed? This is perhaps a proper reply; yet it is difficult not to feel that an object that can exist all over the world in different facts has rather the character of a universal.[3]

I went on to say that this Ramseyesque view was not Wittgenstein's: "it is only the logical network that is 'universal'". But I had no evidence for saying the view was not Wittgenstein's: I mistakenly thought this followed from the fact that "only the 'logical network' was universal".

That is to say, because Ramsey failed to distinguish name and function, I thought that in spite of all he said those objects which, according to him, were represented by functions would *have* to be 'universals'; I did not appreciate the force of his argument that they were no more 'universal' than the bearers of the *names* of the *Tractatus* theory.

Now let us consider the objects covered by 'red' and 'green' in "A is red", "A is green" and "B is red". "Red" and "green" must in any case each cover a *plurality* of objects, for as "material properties" they are "first formed by a configuration" (2.0231). I have also always thought that exactly the same objects were involved in the sense of "A is red" and "A is green": the same objects in a different configuration. This solves the problems raised by the incompatibility of the two propositions.[4] However I did think that the objects covered by "red" in "A is red" and "B is red" would be different where A and B were different, because *the objects must be individuals*. This point is of course independent of the other.

But suppose after all the objects covered by "red" in "A is red" and "B is red" are the same. Does that make them into universals? Well, if it does so simply because they are found in a nexus with A in the one case and B in the

---

[3] *An Introduction to Wittgenstein's Tractatus*, p. 109.

[4] See Edwin Allaire, '*Tractatus*, 6.3751', *Analysis*, 19 (1959).

other, then equally A and B, or the objects constituting them will be universals. That is Ramsey's argument, and it appears to be correct. There is no ground for a distinction of types of object.

But if the features of negatability and of having argument places are what mark the expressions for universals, then these objects will not be universals, even if they do exist separately all over the world at once. "Universal" in this sense is a term applicable only to functions; not to any sort of object. And functions are purely linguistic; nothing in reality except the objects themselves, in logical configuration if they are plural, corresponds to a function; but there is no place in logical enquiry for the question whether functions might or could not 'cover' single names.

Thus far exegesis. It should be clear now, if I am right, that from the *Tractatus* point of view the distinction between individuals and universals – individual things which are the bearers of singular names and universal things which are the bearers of general names – is meaningless. The concept of a universal is a bastard progeny of two quite distinct concepts – those of *function* and of the existence of an object in *many facts*. The former is linguistic; the latter, not peculiar to these objects which are involved in expressions for properties and relations.

It appears to me that the point is of far more than exegetical interest. But for the moment let this suffice.

13 The Question of Linguistic Idealism

I

"If anyone believes that certain concepts are absolutely the right ones, and that having different concepts would mean not realizing something that we realize – then let him imagine certain very general facts of nature to be different from what we are used to, and the formation of concepts different from usual ones will become intelligible to him" (*Philosophical Investigations* [*PI*], II, XII).

This is one of the passages from Wittgenstein arousing – in my mind at least – the question: have we in his last philosphical thought what might be called a linguistic idealism? Linguistic, because he describes concepts in terms of linguistic practices. And he also wrote: "*Essence* is expressed by grammar" (*PI*, I, § 371).

Now, we might accept this dictum in the following way: as Plato suggested in the *Cratylus*, words for the same thing in different languages – e.g. *equus, cheval, horse, ἵππος* – are like the same tool made of different materials, say iron, steel, bronze, brass. A tool which is designed to catch hold of something will perhaps have a shape corresponding to the shape of the object. So a word has something, which we will call its logical shape, answering to the essence that it catches hold of (or expresses). In their sensibly perceptible aspects those words differ from one another; their logical shape is the same. This logical shape is the grammar of the words. This isn't a matter of the most superficial grammatical features, as that the word for something is inflected, or that certain phrases containing the word are compounded in certain ways, as may happen in one language and not in another (as: in English there is or was a call "To horse!") – not a matter of the fine details that would be described by a commentator on Panini. But there is a crude grammar common to all, by which each is e.g. a count-noun which is the name of a kind of whole living thing.

Suppose we accept this last, and do not here pause to show that the fixing of a word as such a word is done by its grammar. But what I mean by "linguistic idealism" would go further and say "Essence is *created* by grammar". For the 'essential' is "the mark of a concept, not the property of an object".[1]

If we assent to "Essence is expressed by grammar" we may very likely say "The words for what I am talking about *have* to have this grammar." E.g.:

---

[1] *Remarks on the Foundations of Mathematics* [*RFM*], I, 73 (any edition). "Mark of a concept" is of course an expression taken from Frege.

From 'Essays on Wittgenstein in honour of G. H. von Wright', *Acta Philosophica Fennica* 28, 1–3, (1976).

The language for talking about sensation must have first–third person asymmetry. But here we don't mean: This property (say, of first–third person asymmetry) is rightly ascribed to this kind of thing (say, sensation). For the property mentioned is a property of language. So we should rather say: Language that doesn't have these features, this grammar, is not about sensations but about something else, and if you took language about sensations and changed this aspect of it, it would cease to be language about sensations. Now language is certainly at least a complicated set of proceedings, mostly with articulate noises. So now it looks as if *either* the grammar corresponded to something of the object, its real essence, which it has whether there is language about it or not, *or* the 'object' were itself dependent on language. The first is like the suggestion made by Plato in the *Cratylus*; the second, if it applies through and through, I call "linguistic idealism".

Going back to my opening quotation: someone might say "I don't want to say that such-and-such concepts are absolutely *the* right ones; I only want to know if they are right ones at all." To take Wittgenstein's own example, in a world where colour and shape were not independent, people might have some colour-shape concepts, and none of colour or of shape. We don't have to suppose, even, that they 'fail to realize what we realize' – e.g. certain similarities of colour. For do we ourselves have a concept wherever we notice a similarity? (See *Zettel*, § 380) What we want to be assured of is that 'what we realize' actually exists and is not a mere projection of the forms of our thinking upon reality.

Wittgenstein appears to suggest that what 'corresponds to' our concept of colour is not (as we might have wished to say) a distinct feature of things, but rather the 'very general fact of nature' that colour and shape are independent.

This suggestion, whatever its merits, is not the suggestion that the essence expressed by the grammar of colour-words is created by that grammar. Yet it does head one off from an attempt to concentrate on and state the essence that the grammar expresses. A scholastic statement about colour, for example, was that it was "whole in the whole, and whole in every part". This would appear in Wittgenstein as, say: "We call something dividing up a square, for example, but nothing dividing up its colour." Or: "Nothing is called a part of red, which appears in one place and is not red, while another part, also not red, appears in another place, so that the two together are said to make up the red." And these are grammatical remarks, remarks about the way in which words are used. "If you talk about essence – you are merely noting a convention" (*RFM*, I, 74).

But now: if we say the essence expressed by the grammar of the word "red" is itself the creation or product of that grammar aren't we saying that nothing would have been red if there had not been human language? If, more particularly, there had not been that linguistic practice with a word, whose existence shows that the users of the word have the concept 'red'. And *that* we do not want to say.

Wittgenstein imagined a tribe with a different concept of pain from ours: their concept applies only where there is visible damage, such as a wound. This is where he answers the question. "But don't they notice the similarity?" (sc. to pain without wounds) by saying "Do we make a concept wherever we see a similarity?" Similarly he says "You learned the *concept* pain when you learned language." That is, it is not experiencing pain that gives you the meaning of the word "pain". How could an experience dictate the grammar of a word? You may say: doesn't it make certain demands on the grammar, if the word is to be the word for *that* experience? But the word is not just a response to that experience at that time: what *else* is the word to apply to? The experience can't dictate what is to be put together with it. "The answer to that is surely: Whatever is the same as it." – What sameness have you in mind? You will say: "The sameness that is expressed by the word." But do you know what sameness that is before you have the word? The experience at any rate does not tell you the limits of use of the word or what sort of instrument it is to be – whether it is to be an exclamation or to have a syntax, for example, and if the latter, whether that of a property of objects perceived. Thus a tribe can be imagined with a different concept of pain, though it overlaps with ours sufficiently to call it that.

Now what is there in all this to make a difficulty about saying: "Even if there had never been any human language so that there *was* 'no concept of pain' at all – still, if there were animals, there would have been pain?" Nothing. – "But which 'pain' are we talking about – pain according to our concept or according to some other possible concept, say the one described?" Well, we are talking our language. So it is pain as we mean "pain" that we are saying would have existed anyway.

And similarly, if there never had been humans around talking about horses, that is not the slightest reason to say there wouldn't have been horses. These essences, then, which are expressed by grammar, are not created by grammar. It must be a misunderstanding of 'essence' to think otherwise: to think, for example, that though there doubtless would have been horses, the essence expressed by "horse" would not have existed but for human language and thought.[2] Could we follow the suggestion of my opening quotation and imagine 'general facts of nature' so different that people did not have the concept 'horse' – although there were horses around? That might be difficult. But when Wittgenstein deprecates thinking that people with different concepts *must* be missing something that we realize, he presumably doesn't mean that they *could* not be supposed to miss something that we realize. It would, rather, be an open question whether they did or not. Suppose, for example, that there were not a great variety of species of mammals, but only horses and humans, and there were no count-noun corresponding to "horse", but some verb form signifying something like horse-presence, we might not find here the concept "horse" and yet we might not

---

[2] Such an error was committed by Locke: according to him essences are general ideas, and general and universal are creations of the mind.

suppose that they 'fail to realize something that we realize'. Or again, having a count-noun, they might apply it to cows on seeing *them.*

I suggested saying that language about sensations had to have a certain grammar – had to have the first–third person asymmetry. But am I not saying *here* that language about horses doesn't have to have the grammar that expresses the essence, horse; e.g. doesn't have to contain a count-noun which is the name of a kind of animal? It seems that I am; should I not then give up my idea about sensations? It seemed that language may at any rate relate to horses without having a word for *a* horse; so may not language similarly relate to sensations without expressing or reporting them? Sensible properties, for example, may be mentioned and scenes described, and the reports be differently treated according as they are first-hand of things currently present to the reporter or as they are second-hand or only remembered, but there are no words for the sense modalities and the words for the sensible properties have no purely 'subjective' use: I mean no use in which they are not subject to correction by other people. The first-hand reports of sensible properties, when counted wrong, are treated as personal stupidity.

To sum up: *Essence is expressed by grammar. But we can conceive of different concepts, i.e. of language without the same grammar. People using this would then not be using language whose grammar expressed the same essences. However, they might not thereby be missing anything that we realize.*

It is enormously difficult to steer in the narrow channel here: to avoid the falsehoods of idealism and the stupidities of empiricist realism.

I understand or mean or think of a kind of animal when I hear, read, or say "horse". But those terms don't signify a mental act such as forming an image or having a representation before me. No image or representation could determine future or past application of the word, i.e. what I and others have called and will call a "horse". *This* is determined by the grammar's expressing an essence. I am master of this grammar: it is by that grammar's expressing an essence that the word I am using means a kind of animal, and hence that *I* mean that. The essence is not what I mean or am speaking of: it is rather that through which I understand or think of (mean) etc. That is to say, it is that because of which my use of the word is a case of meaning a kind of animal. Locke's error was first to think that the 'idea' was the object of thinking; was what a word stands for and so what we mean when we use it, and second to think that when we speak of 'a kind of animal' we must mean a general idea, which he identifies with a 'nominal essence' and calls a creature of the understanding. Whereas, if asked to explain what the word "horse" signifies, we may point to a horse saying "That is a horse" and to another one saying "So is that", from which, if our hearer understands our explanation, he will grasp that the word is the name of a kind. If, then, seeing a donkey, he supposes it too is a horse, he might say "But isn't it the same as you pointed to before?" showing that the identity in question is identity of kind. "Pointing twice to the same" is an expression that does not yet determine what counts as that: the question only has a determinate answer when we know what identity, what method of counting, is relevant. A horse has been counted and another horse comes along; if the procedure is to say "we've counted that one", but to assign a *new* number to, say, a giraffe (a giraffe not having been counted before) – then it appears that one is counting kinds. But what one is counting is in any case out there before one, and not in either case a 'creature of the mind'. If anything is the creation of the mind it is the grammar of one's expressions. If what we mean by "idea" is the essence expressed by that grammar, then in the case of the idea of a horse *that* is no creature of the mind. Nor is it the object of thinking; it is that about the grammar of the word, by which horses are spoken and so also thought of by means of the word. And it is common to otherwise dissimilar words of different languages.

But so powerful is the suggestion of the superficial forms of grammar, that when we speak of 'counting kinds of animal' *as opposed to* 'counting horses' (for note that the former expression is ambiguous), it sounds as if the former expression introduced some new objects to count over and above horses and giraffes and men, for example; as if some new reality were being postulated. Whereas we have only introduced a different way of counting what is before us. It is as with letters on a page. Told to 'count these' one assumes or needs to be told some particular method of counting. With the method is associated a concept C which is used to say 'what' one is counting. Separate marks? Physically separate letters? Letters of the alphabet of distinct type fount? Type founts? Etc. – The rock-bottom explanation of counting each of these is the counting procedures themselves.

When the view is introduced that counting kinds is counting a different sort of objects from counting individuals (for after all, the grammatical object of the verb 'to count' is different!) then of course the question arises: where are some of these objects to be found? In the realm of Platonic forms? In the mind?

It is astonishing how deeply people are sunk in this bog, which is created by pure grammatical misunderstanding. One will not understand Wittgenstein well unless one notices that he has not anywhere so much as got his feet muddied by it. Somewhere in one of his notebooks he wrote: "Numerical identity: a bad concept". As indeed it is; for if you say "same in number", i.e. "same for purposes of counting", the question still is "same *what* in number?" or "same for purposes of counting *how?*" – There is only one letter *e* in the Roman alphabet, for example. Any *e* is numerically the same *letter of the Roman alphabet* as any other. Greek, on the other hand, has two *e*'s – ϵ and η.

The foregoing considerations lead to the following test, if we want to know whether Wittgenstein is a 'linguistic idealist'. We shall ask the question: Does this existence, or this truth, depend upon human linguistic practice? That the *meaning of expressions* is so dependent is evident; that human possession of concepts is so dependent is not quite so evident. A deaf-mute untrained in a language with a syntactical organization or even in any conventional system of signs may have dealings with his fellow-humans which clearly involve his making and complying with varied requests, the earning and spending of money, the response to and joining in various other specially human activities; it is not surprising to learn that such a man can make or laugh at a joke, for example, a visible, acted joke. On the other hand we take it as obvious that there is a host of concepts and considerations which are quite inaccessible to him; also it is fruitless to speculate how much of his capacity is dependent on the existence of the language-using life of those he lives among. The competent use of language is *a* criterion for the possession of the concepts symbolized in it, and so we are at liberty to say: to have such-and-such linguistic practices is to have such-and-such concepts. "Linguistic practice" here does not mean merely the production of words properly arranged into sentences on occasions which we vaguely call "suitable". It is important that it includes activities *other* than the production of language, into which a use of language is interwoven. For example, activities of measuring, of weighing, of giving and receiving and putting into special places, of moving about in a huge variety of ways, of consulting tables and calendars and signs and acting in a way which is connected with that consultation. It is plausible to say that we would have no concept of *length* apart from some activity of measuring, and no concept of precise comparative lengths of distant objects if the activity of measuring had not a quite elaborate use of words interwoven into it.

When Kronecker said "God made the whole numbers, all else is human construction" what can we take him to mean? At first sight, little. Humans would not, I suppose, have had the concept of the natural numbers if they had not had the practice of counting objects. (What do I mean by this? I suppose something like the following: if there isn't a practice of counting objects, it is difficult to see how anything could be identified as a series of natural numbers.) But this fact does not dispose us to think that there could have been no such event as that a wolf killed three deer in seven days, before there were humans with their linguistic practices. So the natural numbers were no more a human invention than wolves, deer, or days. But the same sort of thing holds for facts involving fractions. Why then are *they* more of a human invention than natural numbers?

Did he mean: the natural numbers are (as it were) given: we could do what we liked with them, and mathematical *truths* are human inventions? Humans invented such a thing as 2×2, though they didn't invent 2. And though they didn't invent halves, they invented $\frac{1}{2}$. They invented doing that with the ideas of *one* and of *two* (there was no similar representation of a half in the Roman numeral system[3]) and they invented treating it as a representative of half of anything. They invented treating half as a number. You might say they

---

[3] See Karl Menninger, *Number Words and Number Symbols*, M.I.T. Press, Cambridge Mass., 1969.

invented half's *being* a number. – Probably this is the right direction to look in.

And now this leads us on to the possibility of what we might call a partial idealism. We have agreed (with small reservations) that the existence of human concepts can be somewhat generally equated with the existence of a great variety of human linguistic practices. But that, we have remarked, by no means implies any dependence on human thought and language, on the part of the things that fall under the concepts.

But there are, of course, a great many things whose existence does depend on human linguistic practice. The dependence is in many cases an unproblematic and trivial fact. But in others it is not trivial – it touches the nerve of great philosophical problems. The cases I have in mind are three: namely rules, rights and promises.

With each of these there is associated a certain use of modal notions. Because of the rules of a game, or of any other procedure, you 'have to' do certain things, you 'cannot' do others. When someone has a right to do something, you 'can't' stop him. If you have made a contract, then under the contract you 'have to' do this, or again 'cannot' do that.

Both a rule and a contract, of course, are themselves either possibly or even necessarily linguistic instruments. If one stares at such instruments in a spirit of philosophic enquiry, one may become puzzled at how they can generate necessities. One may then become equally puzzled about what they *are*. It is evident that they contain descriptions of conduct, positive and negative, or descriptions which look like descriptions of states of affairs, such as the membership of a committee. These descriptions may occur in the present or future tense or in a peculiar mood which we may call the mandatory future. Or they may apparently be 'permissive', their main verb being modified by 'may'. But this mandatory or permissive style does not signify that someone is ordering or giving permission to do anything. Were that the situation, the peculiar philosophical problems that arise about rules and promises would not arise. Someone is told to do something by someone else; he gives signs of understanding and he complies or disobeys. That situation we understand.

The case of the promise or contract is different. It is not just a question of a description which someone then makes come true – or else does not. The significance of the promise is the imposition of a kind of necesssity upon him to make the description come true. But what can this necessity be? We may say: it is of either making the description come true, *or* being guilty of an injustice. But what injustice? – That of breaking a promise! Making the promise consisted in giving a sign of generating a new injustice: one of not making a description come true which one was otherwise at perfect liberty not to make come true! That is the meaning of a promise. But how *can* the meaning of a sign be that as a result of its being given, something is to be an offence against its meaning? Its meaning has not properly been explained. This was one of Hume's greatest observations: he called it the "natural unintelligibility" of promises.

Hume divided the problem up into two: first, the problem of meaning, and second, even if we grant there can be such a meaning, of how any 'obligation' could be generated. Now it may seem to be a question how there are *two* distinct problems here. For since the first question was how the meaning of the sign of promising could be *that* by giving it an obligation was generated, it might be thought that if for the sake of the argument it was granted that there *could* be such a meaning, the second question is already answered: if the meaning is that an obligation is generated, then the obligation is generated by the utterance of a sign with the meaning. But Hume is right; the two questions are separate. For let us suppose that instead of promising, I say "Let there be a constraint upon me to act thus and so." *That* of course is perfectly intelligible, since it lacks the peculiar character of the promise by which the sign itself is supposed to be a profession of generating the constraint (obligation). But if I do say that, it will be a question whether there then *does* come about any such constraint. And similarly, even if *per impossibile* the promise was after all 'naturally intelligible', so that the first problem of its meaningfulness was solved, the second question would still arise; does the supposed obligation come about? And if so, how?

Hume's discussion is primarily in terms of the 'act of mind' supposedly expressed by a promise, but the essentials of his argument do not depend on that and are reproduced in such an exposition as I have given. His chapter is celebrated and has led to a large literature on the substantive question: what account to give of promises and the obligation arising from them. Hume's own conclusion was "That promises have no force antecedent to human conventions". If moralists have found this offensive, this will have been by misunderstanding it. The rightness of this conclusion is independent both of Hume's psychology and of his theory of the foundation of morals in a peculiar sentiment. For it can be derived purely from consideration of the meaning problem that he uncovered, and from seeing that here linguistic practice creates the essence which grammar expresses.

We have to draw attention to the use of modals: "must", have to", etc., which is far more extensive than has usually been considered in philosophy. There is a game played with children in which people's hands are successively laid on top of one another. The one whose hand is at the bottom 'has to' pull it out and lay it on top. This is one of the primitive uses of "you have to", it is accompanied by *making* the learner do what he 'has to'. Thus at first, as we might say, he 'literally' has to, that is, he is compelled. But then, if he reacts to the training with human intelligence, the "you have to" itself becomes an instrument of getting him to do such things.

One such use of "you have to" is associated with 'keeping your word', i.e. (in some circumstances) making your word come true. Another is associated with giving details of 'how to' do various sorts of work where others are to learn from your explanation. Another with more or less elaborate performances of a great variety of kinds – games, rituals, etiquette, ceremonious proceedings. Consider the utterance "You have to move your king", said perhaps to a learner in chess. This is indeed equivalent to "The rules of the game require that you move your king". But a child who is learning may not yet grasp the concept: 'The rules of the game require . . .' Accepting "You have to move your king, he's in check", and internalizing such acceptance, is part of learning the concept 'The rules of the game require . . .' 'Requiring' is putting some sort of necessity upon you, and what can that be? In another sense, unless someone compels you, you don't 'have to' move your king. You can easily move another piece instead, for example. "But that wouldn't *be* a move in the game!" True: but that only means: no other move at this point is *called* a "move of the game". Learning the game, learning the very idea of such a game, acquiring the concept of the 'you have to' which is expressed, grasping the idea of a rule: all these hang together, and there isn't a distinct meaning for "being a move in the game" (unless by analogy from other such games) which explains or logically implies the "You have to" which comes into the learning.

The parallel between rules and promises is obscured by the fact that a promise is a sign, whereas we want to say that a rule is not a sign but is rather the meaning of a sign, and that it may be a rule without being formulated. That was why the problem of meaning was felt so acutely in the case of promising; for everyone would agree that the necessity of acting *so* because of a promise was supposed to be generated by its being given. The requirement of acting *so* because of a rule is not generated by the rule's being uttered. Nevertheless the problem is parallel; for the necessity is supposed to be generated by the existence of the rule, and in explaining what a rule is beyond a mere regularity, one will say, e.g., that it is given in a formula for acting, whose meaning is that one must act in accordance with it. And why? Because it is a rule. We move in just such a circle as Hume complained of for promises. Hume might ask what act of mind the assent to a rule is, beyond a resolution to act in a certain regular manner.

Where the regular manner of acting defines a practice, we may avoid the problem by saying that the rules of course don't impose any necessity upon you, except that of acting so *if* you wish to engage in the practice. E.g. if you want to dance a certain dance, you will make the steps and other movements which belong to that dance. Here is a description of the behaviour called "dancing this dance" and you look to the description with a view to making it a true description of your behaviour. But this account neglects the role of rules in a practice in which something's being a rule is supposed to justify or necessitate this action. In the one case it's "If you don't make these steps you won't be doing that dance"; in the other: "If you don't treat these rules as binding, you aren't playing chess." But isn't the latter an odd thing to say – especially if someone *is* only making correct moves? In what move is he 'treating the rules as binding' or failing to do so? The difference will appear in his attitude to 'incorrect' moves. In the dance an incorrect step means that you aren't doing what you are trying to do, and acceptance of it is just not minding doing it wrong or not minding a casual variant. In chess the question would be: "Is he changing the game? If so, what are the new rules?" The incorrect move 'isn't allowed'. The rules *forbid* it. It is this concept that marks something's being treated as a rule rather than as a description of behaviour that you may want to engage in. And it is this that is in Hume's sense 'naturally unintelligible'.

When the rules define a practice which we are free to engage in or not as we like, and of which we may after all construct new variants with different rules, the point excites no anxiety. But when it comes to rules of logic, it is otherwise. Of course if we speak of rules, some people will entertain the idea of constructing variants; and if we speak of logical truths, some people will think of these as perhaps up for revision, on the grounds that anything supposed to be known is supposed to be revisable. Both ideas are a mere distraction. Valid inference, not logical truths, is the subject matter of logic; and a conclusion is justified, not by rules of logic but, in some cases by the truth of its premises, in some by the steps taken in reaching it, such as making a supposition or drawing a diagram or constructing a table. If someone invents variant rules, e.g. a system with more than two truth values, there is the question whether these rules have been followed in some exercise. According to what rules is the deduction, the transition, made from given rules to particular practice? Always there is the logical *must*: you 'can't' have this *and* that; you can't do that if you are going by this rule; you must grant this in face of that. And just as "You can't move your king" is the more basic expression for one learning chess, since it lies at the bottom of his learning the concept of the game and its rules, so these "You must's" and "You can't's" are the more basic expressions in logical thinking. But they are not what Hume calls "naturally intelligible" – that is to say, they are not expressions of perception or experience.[4] They are understood by those of normal intelligence as they are trained in the practices of reasoning.

Another sort of practice with a use of modals interwoven into it generates customary rights such as are to be found in any human society that I ever heard of; the *concept* 'a right' may indeed not exist, but the restriction on doing what it is another's to do (for example) or on preventing him, which are accomplished by the art of linguistic practice – these seem to be found everywhere. The concept 'a right', like that of 'a relation', is the product of sophisticated reflection on the data.

"Is this truth, this existence, the product of human linguistic practice?" This was my test question. I should perhaps have divided it up: Is it so actually? Is it so according to Wittgenstein's philosophy? Now we have partial answers. Horses and giraffes, colours and shapes – the existence of these is not such a product, either in fact or in Wittgenstein. But the metaphysical necessities belonging to the nature of such things – these *seem* to be regarded by him as 'grammatical rules'. "Consider 'The only correlate in language to a necessity of nature is an arbitrary rule. It is the only thing one can milk out of a necessity of nature into a proposition' " (*PI*, I, § 372). This is a form in

---

[4] Hume never saw this: to him inference and judgement and the grasp of a term were all equally 'idea'. See *Treatise of Human Nature* I, III, VII, the long footnote.

which Wittgenstein advances propositions about which he finds *something*
convincing but which he is worried about. *Could* he say that quite generally?
Is it really 'arbitrary'? He always seemed to say in particular cases that
something that appears as a metaphysical necessity is a proposition of
grammar. Is grammar 'arbitrary'? (See his remarks on "Every rod has a
length" [*PI*, I, §251].) However this may be if there is such a thing as idealism
about rules and about the necessity of doing *this* if you are to be in confor-
mity with *this* rule, then here Wittgenstein was a linguistic idealist. He insists
that these things are the creation of human linguistic practice. To repeat, this
does not mean just the practices of arranging words together and uttering
them in appropriate contexts. It refers e.g. to *action* on the rule; actually
going *this* way by the signpost. The signpost or any directive arrow may be in-
terpreted by some new rule. When I see an arrow at an airport pointing ver-
tically upwards, I mentally 'reinterpret' this, and might put my interpretation in the form of another arrow, horizontal and pointing in the direction I
am looking in when I see the first. But the arrows with their interpretations
await action: what one actually does, which is counted as what was meant:
that is what fixes the meaning: And so it is about following the rules of correct
reasoning. One draws the conclusion as one 'must'. That is what "thinking"
means (*RFM*, I, 131). If so, then what will Wittgenstein say about 'illogical'
thinking? As I would, that it isn't thinking? At the Moral Science Club he
once quoted a passage from St Augustine about God which with the
characteristic rhetoric of St Augustine sounded contradictory, Wittgenstein
even took "he moves without moving" as a contradiction in intent, and was
impatient of being told that that at least was not so, the first "moves" being
transitive and the second intransitive (*movet, non movetur*). He wished to take
the contradiction as seriously intended and at the same time to treat it with
respect. This was connected with his dislike of rationality, or would-be
rationality, in religion. He would describe this with a characteristic simile:
there is something all jagged and irregular, and some people have a desire to
encase it in a smooth ball: looking within you see the jagged edges and
spikes, but a smooth surface has been constructed. He preferred it left
jagged. I don't know how to distribute this between philosophical observation on the one hand and personal reaction on the other. In the Catholic
faith, certain beliefs (such as the Trinity, the Incarnation, the Eucharist) are
called "mysteries"; this means at the very least that it is neither possible to
demonstrate them nor possible to show once for all that they are not contradictory and absurd. On the other hand contradiction and absurdity is not
embraced; "This can be disproved, but I still believe it" is not an attitude of
faith at all. So ostensible proofs of absurdity are assumed to be rebuttable,
each one in turn. Now this process Wittgenstein himself once described:
"You can ward off *each* attack as it comes" (Personal conversation). But the
attitude of one who does that, or wishes that that should be done, is not that
of willingness to profess contradiction. On the contrary. On the other hand,
religious mysteries are not a theory, the product of reasoning; their source is

quite other. Wittgenstein's attitude to the whole of religion in a way assimilated it to the mysteries: thus he detested natural theology. But again, what part of this was philosophical (and therefore something which, if right, others ought to see) and what part personal, it is difficult to say. In natural theology there is attempted reasoning from the objects of the world to something outside the world. Wittgenstein certainly worked and thought in a tradition for which this was impossible. If something is a logical inference,[5] then "no experience can contradict the conclusion without contradicting the premises. But that means that you are moving about within your means of representation" (*RFM*, 2nd edn, VII, 25).

The last statement is not precise, but doesn't it imply the 'no new information' thesis about logical inference (narrowly construed)? Elsewhere (*RFM*, 2nd edn, VII, 64), Wittgenstein proposed the following: if one could learn to characterize the presence and absence of colours by truth-functional formulae like "Either no green, or white", might there not be three distinct observations which would correspond to an inconsistent triad of such formulae? But if they are distinct observations, then it must be possible that all of them should occur. The 'no new information' thesis could hardly be put more strongly: that is to say, just because a logical conclusion contradicted a possible distinct observation, he is willing rather to allow that an actual observation may contradict another actual observation, than to allow that one observation should – logically – *exclude* another. But might it not be that *we* don't let any situation be characterized as one in which there are these three – accurate – observations? Of course we have 'means of representation' at our disposal here: we can talk of 'appearances'; aren't there even *single* impressions, and pictures, of impossible states of affairs? And so in fact Wittgenstein's characterization of the three 'observations' would be challenged. But he could deny that this was a case of rightly claiming to derive new information; of 'logic dictating' what an observation must be. For he could say what I just said. Logic then dictates our refusal to *call* something an "observation".

The dependence of logical possibility on grammar, and the arbitrariness that then seems to belong to what is counted as logically possible, are canvassed in the following passage: "If a proposition is conceived as a picture of a possible state of affairs and said to show its possibility, still it can at most do what a painting or relief or film does: and so at any rate it can't put there what is not the case. [I take this to mean: what is not the case, if what it represents *is* the case.] So does it depend wholly on our grammar what will be called (logically) possible and what not – i.e. what that grammar permits?" – But that is surely arbitrary! – Is it arbitrary? – It is not every sentence-like formation that we know how to do something with, not every technique has its application in our life; and when we are tempted in philosophy to count

---

[5] I should stress that my considerations here *only* concern Wittgenstein's attitude to logic – to logical inference as a practice – and do not deal with his views on mathematics, which are far more complex. For it is obvious that mathematics is a huge structure, or complex of structures.

some quite useless thing as a proposition, that is often because we have not considered its application sufficiently (*PI*, I, §520).

The non-arbitrariness of logic, therefore, is not a way of 'bargaining its rigour out of it' (*PI*, I, §108). And yet it, with its rigour, is quite clearly regarded as a linguistic creation.

Wittgenstein invites us to compare 'logically possible' with 'chemically possible'. A compound might be called chemically possible if a formula with the right valencies existed, e.g. H-O-O-O-H. "Of course the compound need not exist, but even a formula HO_2 can't have less than no compound corresponding to it in reality" (*PI*, I, §521). This is an interesting illustration. The notation enables us to construct the formula HO_2, but the system then rules it out. Impossibility even has a certain role: one examines a formula to see that the valencies are right. The exclusion belongs to the system, a human construction. It is objective; that is, it is not up to me to decide what is allowable here.

II

This leads us on to another way of raising the question of a sort of idealism. "So you are saying that human agreement decides what is true and what is false? – It is what humans *say* that is true and false, and they agree in the *language* they use. That is not agreement in opinions . . ." (*PI*, I, § 241). What are the implications of 'agreement in language'?

It runs through Wittgenstein's thought that you haven't got a *mistake* just because you have as a complete utterance a string of words contrary to one in which some truth is expressed. I can be accused of *making a mistake* when I know what it is for a given proposition (say) to be true, and things aren't like that but I suppose that they are. (There is a corresponding condition for being right.) This means that I have to be actually operating the language.[6] My proceedings with it have to belong in the system of thought that is in question. Otherwise such an utterance may be nothing at all; it may be 'superstition' (*PI*, I, §110) or 'a queer reaction' or a manifestation of some different 'picture of the world', or of a special form of belief which flies in the face of what would be understood to falsify it but for its peculiarity; it may be some strange secondary application of words; it may be a mere manifestation of ignorance like a child's. It may be madness. But in none of these cases is Wittgenstein willing to speak of a 'mistake'.

That is not to say that he never sees grounds for criticism. To say something is 'superstition – not mistake' is certainly a reproach. It was a criticism of a particular kind of philosophic thought. What he calls a 'mistake' is something for which there are unsatisfied criteria of correctness, criteria which correspond to the intention of the speaker. (In this sense Aristotle might have called Plato's Theory of Forms "superstition, not mistake": superstition "itself produced by grammatical illusions".

---

[6] *On Certainty* [*Cert.*], § 676: He who says "I'm dreaming" in a dream, even speaking audibly, is no more right than when in a dream he says "It's raining" while it actually is raining.

Now our question is: outside this one example, does Wittgenstein's view preclude our saying "They are utterly wrong, they are in darkness?" Does it preclude objecting to e.g. a different picture of the world, such as is evinced by the Aztecs in their quinquagesimal fear that the course of nature would change? Or a strange belief like those of Tibetan Lamaism? Or to magical beliefs and practices? Of course, in one way it can't preclude objecting; but does it preclude having grounds, being right?

As readers of the 'Notes on Frazer' will know, Wittgenstein rejected the idea that 'our science' shows that magical practices and beliefs are errors. Above all, he thought it stupid to take magic for mistaken science. Science can correct only scientific error, can detect error only in its own domain; in thoughts belonging to its own system of proceedings. About the merits of other proceedings it has nothing to say except perhaps for making predictions.

Talking about these matters I once asked Wittgenstein whether, if he had a friend who went in for witch-doctoring, he would want to stop him. He thought about this for a little and said "Yes, but I don't know why." I believe that the objection is a religious one. A scientist cannot condemn superstitious practices on the basis of his science. He may do so on the basis of a 'scientistic' philosophy. But there is no need for him to hold such a philosophy in order to pursue his science. Now it is clear that Wittgenstein himself did not hold such a philosophy and did not think it belonged to respect for science and interest in scientific matters to do so. In his work up to *On Certainty* we might think we could discern a straightforward thesis: there can be no such thing as 'rational grounds' for our criticizing practices and beliefs that are so different from our own. These alien practices and language games are simply there. They are not ours, we cannot move in them.

In *On Certainty* Wittgenstein was led to consider Moore's claim to know, among other things, that he had never been far from the surface of the earth, and that the earth had existed for a long time before he was born. Wittgenstein's considerations about never having been on the moon have constituted a fool-trap which a surprising number of people have fallen into. At the date at which he wrote the certainty of never having been on the moon was altogether different from, say, the certainty of never having been in China. " 'I *know* I have never been on the moon'. That sounds quite different in the circumstances which actually hold, to the way it would sound if some men had been on the moon, and some perhaps without knowing it. In *this* case one could give grounds for this knowledge . . . I want to say: my not having been on the moon is as sure a thing for me as any grounds I could give for it" (Cert., §111). The situation he imagined in this remark has come about; but that should not incapacitate his readers! What he wrote was true when he wrote it, and was not supposed to be necessarily true for all times.

In 1871 a Russian explorer, Nikolai Miklouho-Maclay, visited New Guinea and thereafter lived there for two periods (1871–2, 1876–7) of more than a year each. He had a Polynesian servant who died, and whom he buried at sea. When the people asked where the man was, he gestured towards the horizon. They, it is said, believed that he meant that the man had flown away over the sea. They also believed that Maclay himself had come from the moon. He told them that he was a man from a place called Russia, and so they supposed that Russia was in the moon. They held a meeting of senior people to ask him questions, among which was "whether he could or would ever die".[7]

It is a similar tribe that Wittgenstein imagines in the following:

> I could imagine Moore being captured by a wild tribe and their expressing the suspicion that he has come from somewhere between the earth and the moon. Moore tells them that he knows etc. but he can't give them the grounds for his certainty, because they have fantastic ideas of human ability to fly and know nothing about physics. This would be an occasion for making that statement (*Cert.*, § 264).

That is, the statement: "I *know* that never . . ." *Here*, Moore has a real occasion for saying that. Wittgenstein goes on to ask: "But what does it say, beyond 'I have never been to such and such a place, and have compelling grounds for believing that'? And here one would have to say what are compelling grounds" (*Cert.*, §§ 264–5). Now compelling grounds are objective (*Cert.*, § 271); in the sense that it is not up to me to decide what is a telling ground (*Cert.*, § 272).

> What we believe depends on what we learn. We all believe that it's not possible to go to the moon; but there might be people who believe that it is possible and that it sometimes happens. We say: these people do not know a lot that we know. And, let them be never so sure of their belief – they are wrong and we know it.
>
> If we compare our system of knowledge with theirs, then theirs is evidently by far the poorer one. (*Cert.*, § 286)

Now let us contrast these passages with the following ones, also from *On Certainty*, which are on the same theme but have important differences and a different moral:

> Suppose some adult had told a child that he had been on the moon. The child tells me the story, and I say it was only a joke, the man hadn't been on the moon; no one has ever been on the moon; the moon is a long way off and it is impossible to climb up there or fly there. – If now the child insists, saying perhaps there is a way of getting there which I don't know, etc. what reply could I make to him? What reply could I make to the adults of a tribe who believe that people sometimes go to the moon (perhaps that is how they interpret their dreams), and who indeed grant that there are no ordinary means of climbing up to it or flying there? – But a child will not ordinarily stick to such a belief and will soon be convinced by what we tell him seriously.
>
> Isn't this altogether like the way one can instruct a child to believe in a God, or

---

[7] See Peter Lawrence, *Road Belong Cargo*, Manchester, 1964. *We* know that those people were fantastically wrong, that there is no question of its being possibly true that Maclay was ever on the moon.

that none exists, and it will accordingly be able to produce apparently telling grounds of the one or the other?

But is there then no objective truth? Isn't it true, or false, that someone has been on the moon? If we are thinking within our system, then it is certain that no one has ever been on the moon. Not merely is nothing of the sort ever seriously reported to us by reasonable people, but our whole system of physics forbids us to believe it. For this demands answers to the questions "How did he overcome the force of gravity?" "How could he live without an atmosphere?" and a thousand others which could not be answered. But suppose that instead of all these answers we met the reply: "We don't know *how* one gets to the moon, but those who get there know at once that they are there; and even you can't explain everything." We should feel ourselves intellectually very distant from someone who said this. (*Cert.*, §§ 106–8)

There is a great difference between the tribe described in § 106 and the tribe that captured Moore in § 264. In one case Wittgenstein says "He can't give them the grounds"; in the other: "What reply could I make?" But here it isn't that he can't 'give them the grounds'; those grounds pass them by, don't convince them. (And they mean something different by 'getting' to the moon from what he would mean.)[8] The grounds were not beyond their grasp – which was why Moore couldn't explain to the savage tribe. And similarly for the man in § 108 who says "We don't know *how* one gets to the moon, but those who get there know at once that they are there, and even you can't explain everything." Wittgenstein comments: "We should feel ourselves intellectually very distant from someone who said this." But there's no refuting such a man. What count as reasons for us, do not count for him. We may 'just have to put up with it' (*Cert.*, § 258). This is because (a) there is a gap between reasons and conviction. Reasons, like explanations, justifications, interpretations of a rule, come to an end – and then one is convinced, or one acts, goes *this* way. And (b) because this is *not* one of those cases where "if someone gives signs of doubt where we do not doubt, we cannot confidently understand his signs as signs of doubt" (*Cert.*, § 154). Not a case where the hypothesis that someone believes something can't be sustained, because we wouldn't know what to identify as someone's believing that. And not a case where the mere idea of accepting *this* (namely what he thinks) destroys the whole business of judging anything.

Let us consider the child who goes on believing the story in § 106. Wittgenstein asks: "What reply could I make to him?" – the same question as in the case of the tribe. There is no demonstration against him. But a child is not as strong as a tribe, is more malleable and "will not stick to such a belief, but soon be convinced by what we tell him seriously". – What do we 'tell him seriously'? That it's all nonsense and *that these grounds* were *sufficient*

---

[8] It changes the situation once people have gone to the moon by spacerocket, and the people of the strange tribe know this. Various developments are possible: they wonder if they will ever meet the cosmonauts on the moon. Or: they dismiss the idea of such an encounter as a misunderstanding. Etc.

for saying so? Why can't we say that to the man? In his case, it seemed, we 'had to put up with it'.

Suppose I were to say: "Wittgenstein, you show quite clearly that that would be lying to the child." Could he reply: "No more than I lie to a child whom I teach arithmetic, and insist that he see only *this* as the way of following a given rule"? He could not fairly make that reply. Just that *was* learning to follow rules. The "must" in "You see, if this is the rule, you must do this here" was itself the creation of language, and the child's acquisition of this 'must' is, as we have seen, part and parcel of its acquiring concepts and practices which it belongs to the human intelligence to have. But the same thing can't be said *here*.

What then? Are we *not* to tell him 'seriously' not to believe the story? Are we to encourage him to 'have an open mind', to work out every possible conception and entertain every strange possibility? Absurd! That idea is based on a false picture of how people can learn; of how they can become competent to entertain all sorts of possibilities. No; we tell him not to believe the story, and we give the reasons: we thereby tell him implicitly not to form and stick to an idea of getting to the moon for which *those* grounds against its having happened would be irrelevant. Or again: we tell him that there is (can be) no truth in the story, and that is an implicit directive not to believe it and not form such an idea.

§107: The comparison with "the way one can instruct a child to believe in a God or that none exists" derives its interest from the rest of the paragraph: "and it will accordingly be able to produce apparently telling grounds for the one or the other". Examining the parallel, we can find an analogue for the objection to the story of the man who had been on the moon. The child has heard that someone made the world, keeps it going and runs it. The objection is that of Lucretius:

> Quis regere immensi summam, quis habere profundi
> Indu manu validas potis est moderanter habenas?

Namely "Who could – i.e. how could anyone – possibly do so?" – There was no analogue in the moon story for the 'apparently telling grounds' on the other side.

It is at any rate clear that this is a quite different treatment of "No one has been on the moon" from the case of the savage tribe. *They* had a poor system of knowledge. These people might not: they might have the same *physics* as we do. What has physics to do with transport to the moon in dreams?

Turning now to the example of the earth's having existed for a long time:

> I can imagine a man who had grown up in quite special circumstances and been taught that the earth came into existence 50 years ago, and therefore believed this. We might teach him that the earth has already . . . for a long time – We should be trying to give him our picture of the world.
>
> This would happen through a kind of persuasion. (*Cert.*, § 262)

This idea of one's 'picture of the world' did not come into play in the same way in Wittgenstein's considerations about never having been on the moon, never having been very far from the earth's surface. For about that he says "What could induce me to believe the opposite? Either a memory, or having been told. – Everything I have seen or heard gives me the conviction that no man has ever been far from the earth. Nothing in my picture of the world speaks in favour of the opposite" (*Cert.*, § 93). That is, it is not an actual part of his 'picture of the world' – that "inherited background against which I distinguish between true and false" (*Cert.*, § 94) *that* he had not, that no one had, been far from the earth. On the other hand the statement that someone had done so raised difficulties from his *system of knowledge*. The 'picture of the world' is not the same thing as the 'system of knowledge'. But there are connections: the 'picture of the world' acquired by the man in the paragraph I have just quoted could hardly co-exist with our physics, and a picture that couldn't co-exist with our physics might well facilitate a belief in some people's visiting the moon. But our teaching of that man will presumably be primarily of history: "The earth has been inhabited for a long, long time. We know what people have been doing for thousands of years. Here are the buildings that were built hundreds of years ago. Etc."

In another passage Wittgenstein imagines Moore arguing with a king who was brought up to believe that the world began with him.

> Could Moore really prove his belief to be the right one? I do not say Moore could not convert the king to his own view, but it would be a conversion of a special kind: the king would be brought to look at the world in a different way.
>
> Remember that one is sometimes convinced of the *correctness* of a view by its *simplicity* or *symmetry*, i.e. these are what induce one to go over to this point of view. One then simply says something like "That's how it *must* be". (*Cert.*, § 92)

This is again different from the case of the previous man (and indeed from the man at the beginning of the same paragraph). For this king has been brought up to believe, not just that the *earth* has existed for only a short time, but that *the world began with him*. That is, *he* is given a superlative position in the world. And if Moore converts him, he is brought to 'see the world in a different way'. This is not just the same thing as his 'being given our picture of the world' perhaps in connection with learning our physics. He could perhaps be given *that* and still retain the idea of his superlative position. *When* did he come to be? If, in the conception of himself that he has been given, he has lived only as long as his apparent age, then there is a peculiar line drawn at a recent date. What *we* would say happened before his time, to him is part of the scene that came into being with him. If the scene in various ways included suggestions of a past, that 'past' was supposed to be merely part of the scene as it came into being then – as Philip Gosse thought the fossils were created in the rocks in 4004 BC. The king's rejection of this base line and of such a position for himself in the world is rightly described as 'conversion'. And these considerations show why Wittgenstein should make those remarks about simplicity and symmetry. The other men who believed that the earth had only existed for a short time were comparable to the savage tribe. Their knowledge system would be very poor. But this king's knowledge system need not be poor at all. May not the Dalai Lama learn our physics and astronomy and history, and yet go on believing that he *is* the same person as all the previous Dalai Lamas?

A main theme of *On Certainty* is the 'groundlessness' of one's world-picture. Finding grounds, testing, proving, reasoning, confirming, verifying are all processes that go on *within*, say, one or another living linguistic practice which we have. There are assumptions, beliefs, that are the 'immovable foundation' of these proceedings. By this, Wittgenstein means only that they are a foundation which is not moved by any of these proceedings. I cannot doubt or question anything unless there are some things I do not doubt or question – e.g. that I know the meaning of some of the words that I use, that if I need to check on others by looking them up in a dictionary, I really am using a dictionary, and so on. And among these would be such facts as belong to my 'picture of the world' – e.g. that it makes sense to ask whether such-and-such a volcano was active a thousand years ago.

Not everything that is 'unmoved' is a foundation. Again, there are some propositions which are quite solid for me, but I do not learn them explicitly:

> I can discover them like the axis around which a body rotates. This 'axis' is not fixed in the sense that anything holds it fast, but the movement around it determines its immobility.
>
> No one ever taught me that my hands don't disappear when I am not paying attention to them. (*Cert.*, §§152–3)

I want to say: we should not regard the struggling investigations of *On Certainty* as all saying the same thing. Doubts whether this is a tree or whether his name was L. W. or whether the world has existed a long time or whether the kettle will heat on the fire or whether he had never been to the moon are themselves not all subjected to the same treatment. Not all these things, for example, are part of a 'world-picture'. And a world-picture is not the same thing as a religious belief, even though to believe is not in either case to surmise. Wittgenstein thought of a motto once: "I'll show you differences." We cannot get him right, but only commit frightful confusions, by making assimilations.[9]

But to return to the question with which I started: it may seem that if ever

---

[9] Thus Norman Malcolm in his paper "The Groundlessness of Belief", which contains a fine exposition of some of Wittgenstein's thought and an interesting thesis about the 'pathology of philosophy', spoils everything by assimilating religious belief, belief in one's 'world-picture', belief in a system of knowledge, *and* the confident action of a shopkeeper serving one with apples. Wittgenstein wrote: "If the shopkeeper wanted to investigate each of his apples without any reason, in order to be certain of what he was doing, why doesn't he (then) have to investigate the investigation? And can one now speak of believing here (I mean in the sense of religious belief, not surmise)? All psychological words here distract from the main point." (*Cert.*, §459) His answer to "Can one now speak of believing here?" is rather plainly "Don't".

world-pictures are incompatible, Wittgenstein rejects the idea of one of them's being right, the other wrong. A world-picture partly lies behind a knowledge system. One knowledge system may be far richer than another, just as it may be connected with far greater capacities of travel, for example. But when, speaking with *this* knowledge system behind one, one calls something error which *counts as knowledge* in another system, the question arises: has one the right to do that? Or has one to be 'moving within the system' to call anything error? "Even if I came to a country where they believed that people were taken to the moon in dreams, I couldn't say to them 'I have never been to the moon – Of course, I may be mistaken.' And if they asked 'May you not be mistaken?' I should have to answer: No." (*Cert.*, § 667). That is to say: even if he might come to count the idea of visits to the moon when dreaming as possibly part of their system of *knowledge*, even then he could not call his present view of the hypothesis that he'd been on the moon a *mistake*. Now is that a personal profession or a logical point? Certainly it is the latter. But, "If we call [what they think] 'wrong', doesn't that mean that we are starting out from our language-game and *combating* theirs?"[10] This is put as a question, but his answer is clearly "Yes", for this has to be the back-reference of "I said I would 'combat' the other man – but wouldn't I give him *reasons*? Certainly, but how far do they go? At the end of reasons comes persuasion." (*Cert.*, § 612)

So what is in question here is not: cultural relativism. For the assumption is of "two principles which really meet and can't be reconciled" and "each man declares the other a fool and heretic" (*Cert.*, § 611). That is to say, we have a "disagreement in the language they use" – but it really is a disagreement. The conflict between the principles of Western medicine and acupuncture medicine might serve as a good example here. But how can it help us with our problem to say "At the end of reason comes *persuasion*"? Is it futile to say here: But won't the persuasion be right or wrong, an intellectual disaster or intellectual enlightenment?

Or is it really another form of: Rules, with their interpretations, cannot finally dictate how you go, can't tell you what is the next step in applying them? In the end you take the rule *this* way, not in the sense of an interpretation, but by acting, by taking the step. Rules and the particular rule are defined by practice: a rule doesn't tell you how you 'must' apply it; intepretations, like reasons, give out in the end. – In all this I did see *a sort of* 'linguistic idealism'.

NO! – It is not the same. For those were cases where the 'doubt', which in fact, of course, I hardly ever have as I apply a rule, has no real content, and disagreement is just imagined by the philosopher. Thus the assumption of Descartes' deceiving demon is not indeed excluded: "If I were to awake from the enchantment I should say 'Why, was I *blind*!' " (cf. *RFM*, I, 135–6). Similarly he entertains the same sort of idea about things like knowing his own name, about which "If that's wrong, I'm crazy" (*Cert.*, § 572), yet: *might* I

---

[10] *Cert.*, § 609. The reference here is to people who consult oracles instead of physicists.

not wake up, have my eyes opened, have to learn from 'a higher authority'? (*Cert.*, § 578).

But the doubt is empty: "What difference does it make for me to 'assume' this [the deceiving demon]? I might say "Yes, sure, the calculation is wrong – but that's how I calculate" (*RFM*, I, 135–6). He could say the same in the case of knowing his own name. It is only in face of the 'presumptuous' use of "know" by Moore that he wants to exclaim: "You don't *know* anything!" (*Cert.*, § 407) "When one hears Moore say "I *know* that that's a tree" one suddenly understands those who think that that hasn't been made out at all. . . . It is as if 'I know' does not tolerate a metaphysical emphasis" (*Cert.*, §§ 481–2).

In short, these were illegitimate doubts. He concedes them only in face of a false picture of legitimate certainty. They are unreal; but they would legitimately arise if the false picture were true. (Like the doubt whether another means the same as I by "red", which is aroused by the picture of the private object.)

It is quite otherwise *either* when there is a conflict of irreconcilable principles in real life, *or* again when I have said "I can't be wrong" about the kind of thing I have a right to say it about – and now it actually looks as if I *were* wrong (*Cert.*, § 641). The situation terminates, in the one case in persuasion, in the other in decision. And now isn't it as if Wittgenstein were saying: there isn't a right or wrong – but only the conflict, or persuasion, or decision?

Suppose he has said "I can't be making a mistake" – of course, in the sort of case where that's an appropriate expression.

> Certainly one can imagine cases, and there are cases, where, after 'waking up' one never doubts again which was fancy and which was reality. But such a case, or its possibility, does not discredit the sentence "I can't be making a mistake".
>
> Otherwise wouldn't it discredit all assertion?
>
> I can't be making a mistake – but I may indeed sometime, rightly or wrongly, believe I realize that I was not competent to judge. (*Cert.*, §§ 643–5)

" . . . rightly or wrongly . . ." – that is the hard part. That I may come to think I was wrong, not competent to judge, is not news. But to say *I can't be making a mistake* and yet to add: I may *rightly* or wrongly come to believe I wasn't competent to judge – isn't that saying "I can't be wrong, yet I may be wrong"? The distinction between *mistake* and something else that can't be called "mistake" just rescues us from the contradiction. But – how much use is that? "I can't be making a mistake" expresses certainty: doesn't that consort ill with the thought, "I may – rightly – come to believe I wasn't competent to judge"? True, I don't usually look at that possibility. But I can't deny it. NB: this is "may", and not "might". The argument from mere conceivability leads only to empty, ornamental doubt, as in face of the idea of the deceiving demon. But here, certainty is defended in face of 'legitimate' doubt (*Cert.*, § 375).

In the next entry (*Cert.*, § 646) the two phenomena are contemplated just as phenomena: the "I can't be making a mistake" and the coming to believe (rightly or wrongly) that I was then not competent to judge. Wittgenstein now makes the observation: "If that always or often occurred, that would indeed completely change the character of the language-game."

With that observation, this particular battle has been fought out. The conclusion is not an idealistic one. *That one knows something is not guaranteed by the language-game.* To say it was, would be linguistic idealism with a vengeance. But here Wittgenstein has at last succeeded in his difficult enterprise, he has attained 'realism without empiricism' (*RFM*, third edn, VI, 23).

That one knows something is not guaranteed by the language-game. This is so, even though there are occasions on which, if someone with our normal education says "I don't know . . ." (e.g. "I don't know if there ever was such a person as Queen Victoria"), one would want to ask: What do you mean? How are you using the word "know"? What would you *call* "knowing that"? This explains why Wittgenstein sometimes dwells on the possibility of substituting "I believe . . ." for "know" in such cases, or always putting it in front of one's assertions, and asks "How much difference would that make?" But *still*: it is "always by favour of Nature that one knows something" (*Cert.*, § 505). But the 'language-game' of assertion, which for speaking humans is so important a part of the whole business of knowing and being certain, depends for its character on a 'general fact of nature'; namely that that sequence of phenomena is rare.

The case of conflict remains unfinished business.

Index

acknowledgement, Brentano's
    conception, xi
'act of mind', Hume's discussion, 119
action,
    Aristotle, 69, 73–5, 77
    Brentano, 100, 106–7
    defined in terms of deliberation, 48
    rules and, 122, 131
addition, 16; *see also* numbers
affirmation, Aristotle, 44–9
agreement, language and, 124
Anaxagoras, 14
annihilation, matter and, 60
antiphasis, Aristotle, 44, 48, 49, 52
Aquinas, St Thomas, x, 74
    necessity and truth, 81–5
Aristotelian Scholastics, 22
Aristotle, x, xi, 84, 107, 124
    De Interpretatione, 44–55
    desire, 102
    early theory of forms, 13, 15, 16–17,
        20, 23
    knowledge, 81, 83
    principle of individuation, 57–65
    revised theory of forms, 32
    theory of categories, 103
    thought and action in, 66–77
arithmetic, 18; *see also* mathematics,
    numbers
assertion,
    'language-game', 133
    predication and, 100
assimilation, between will and
    emotion, 101, 106
asymmetry, first–third person, 113, 115
atomism, retreat from, 84
Augustine, St, 101–2, 122
Ayer, A. J., 81, 83

becoming, relation of monads to
    infinitude of, 24n
being,
    Parmenides, viii–ix

Plato, x, 21–3, 25, 27–31
belief,
    in history, 89
    learning and, 126, 128, 133
    positiveness of, 103
    understanding and, 36–9
Boethius, Anicius, 82
Brentano, Franz, xi, 85
    will and emotion, 100–102, 104–6

Caesar, Julius, Hume on, 86–91
calculation, Aristotle, 66
categories, Aristotle's theory of, 103
causality,
    Brentano, 106
    early theory of forms, 14–15
    Hume's principle of, 93–4
cause,
    and beginning of existence, 93–4
    early theory of forms, 15
    and effect, 86–8, 96–8, 106
Cebes, 14
certainty,
    'demonstrably certain', 93
    'intuitively certain', 93
    language and, 132
    cf. truth, 51, 52, 54
change, matter and, 59–60
chemical elements, matter and, 58
'chemically possible', 124
choice, Aristotle, 66–71, 73, 76–7, 102
Cicero, 91
class, concept of, cf. Platonic form,
    11–14 17, 26, 33
collections, classes as, 12
colour, and sight, 40–42
combinability of number, 17–18
concept,
    and linguistic idealism, 113, 117–18,
        120–21
    'metaphysical', 57–8
    and object, 108–9
conclusion, and premise, 15

consequences, confusion with
   principles, 15
contingency, Aquinas, 81
contract, language and, 118
contradiction,
   Aquinas, 83
   Parmenides, 3–8
   religion and, 122
   revised theory of forms, 32
conviction, reasons and, 127
Copi, Irving, 108
corruption, 23, 24
count-noun, 114–15
counting, *see also* numbers
   language and, 116–17
Cratylus (Plato), 112, 113
Cyropaedeia (Xenophon), 90

De Anima (Aristotle), 74, 75
De Civitate Dei (Augustine), 101
De Generatione et Corruptione (Aristotle),
   64
De Interpretatione (Aristotle), 44–55
De Rerum Natura (Lucretius), 90
decision,
   language and, 132
   reached by deliberation, 67–8, 70
definition, form and, 62–4
deliberation,
   action defined in terms of, 48
   Aristotle, 66–72
Descartes, René, xi, 3, 131
description, definite, 63
descriptive terms, xi
desire,
   Aristotle, 66, 72, 75
   and will, 101, 102, 104
Development of Logic, The (Kneale and
   Kneale), 16, 16n
dialectic, Aristotle, 46, 48
dialectical science, Plato, 32–3
difference, and Plato's theory of
   forms, 29
Diodorus Cronus, x, 56
distress, will and, 101
divine knowledge of the future,
   Aquinas' discussion of, x
division,
   early theory of forms, 16

revised theory of forms, 27
'doing well', Aristotle, 69, 71, 75, 76–7

effect, cause and, 86–8, 93–4, 96–8, 106
emotions, 85
   will and, 100–107
empiricism, realism without, 133
essence, expressed by grammar,
   112–14, 114n, 115–16, 119
eternity, 82
Ethics (Aristotle), 66
evil, 104, 107
exclusion, and revised theory of
   forms, 31
existence,
   Aristotle, 48, 49
   cause and beginning of, 93–9
   concept of intentional, 85
   and thought, 3–8
expectation, 102
experience,
   belief in matters outside, 86
   language and, 121
explanation, language and, 119
Extensionality, Law of, 11–12

falsity, Aristotle, 44, 45, 49
Faust (Goethe), 103
fear, and will, 101, 102
feeling, and will, 105, 106
forms,
   as beings, ix
   early theory of, 9–20
   Platonic, 9–20, 116, 124
   principle of individuation, 57,
      61–3, 65
   revised theory of, 21–33
Foundations of Arithmetic (Frege), 16
fractions, 117
Frege, Gottlob, 16, 112n
   concept and object, 108–9
   predication and assertion, 100
   revised theory of forms, 26–7
function, name and, 108, 110–11
future,
   Aquinas, 81
   Aristotle, 46
   divine knowledge of the, x
future contingents, x

future contingents—*cont.*
  Aquinas, 82–3
future time reference, Aristotle, 49,
  52, 54–5

Galen, 91
Geach, P., 65n, 103
generation, 23, 24
genus–species division, 33
geometry,
  early theory of forms, 18, 20
  Meno, 34–5
given, notion of the, 84
Goethe, Johann Wolfgang von, 103
good, Brentano, 104, 107
Gosse, Philip, 129
grammar, and linguistic idealism,
  112–16, 119, 122–3
growth, 64–5

Hartley, M., 49n
hate, 103
Hegel, Georg Wilhelm, 84
history, 89, 91
Hobbes, Thomas, 95
hope, expectation and, 102–3
Hume, David, xi, 121n
  Aristotle and, 75
  beginning of existence and cause,
    93–9
  cause and effect, 86–90
  'natural unintelligibility' of promises,
    118–19, 120–21
hypothesis, 'strongest available', 15
  cf. principle, 19, 20
hypothetical argument, Hume, 87–8

idea,
  essence as general, 114n, 115, 116
  Hume's doctrine of abstract, 98
  separable, 96
idealism, xi
  linguistic, 112–33
identity,
  language and, 115–16
  numerical, 116–17
  and principle of individuation,
    62, 64–5
imaginability, of beginning of

existence, 96–8
imagination, and judgement, 100
impossible, can't clearly be conceived
  to be, 3
incompatability, and revised theory
  of forms, 32
individual,
  counting, 116
  indefinable, 62, 64
  and universal, 108, 110–11
individuation, principle of, 57–65
inexpressibility, 8
inference,
  of cause from effect, 86–9, 93
  language and, 121, 121n, 123, 123n
intellect, choice and, 69
intelligence, 107
intercommunion of forms, doctrine
  of, 23, 24, 25, 26
interpretation, language and, 131

joy, will and, 101
judgement,
  choice and, 69, 76–7
  imagination, 100
'just itself', Plato, 23

Kant, Immanuel, 59, 84, 106
Katz, Dr Stephen, 88n
'keeping your word', language and,
  119
kinds, counting, 116
Kneale, M., 16n
Kneale, W. C., 15, 16n
knowledge, viii, 13, 106
  Aquinas, 82–3
  and early theory of forms, 9, 13–14
  is of changelessly true, 81
  Meno, 34, 40, 41
  Moore, 132
  system of, 129–31, 133
  cf. truth, 51, 54
  and understanding, 40–42

language, xi
  linguistic idealism, 112–33
Language, Truth and Logic (Ayer), 81
Lawrence, Peter, 126n
learning,

learning—*cont.*
  and belief, 126
  understanding and, 41
Leibniz, 94
length, measuring and, 117
Locke, John, 114n, 115
logic, 109
  Joseph, 57
  language and, 121, 123, 123n, 124
  necessity and, 49
'logically possible', 124
love, objects of, 103–4
Lucretius, 90, 128
Łukasiewicz, Jan, 57, 57n, 59, 60–62

Maclay, N. M., 125–6, 126n
magic, 125
Malcolm, Norman, 130n
"many", and revised theory of forms,
  26–7
Marcus Aurelius, 91
'mark of a concept', 112, 112n
material difference, 64; *see also* matter
mathematical objects, 'intelligible
  matter' and, 63
mathematics,
  and early theory of forms, 17–20
  language and, 117–18, 123n
  Meno, 34, 39–40
matter,
  'intelligible', 63
  'matter in itself', 59
  principle of individuation, 57–65
  'undesignate', 61
meaning, 116
  language and, 119–20, 122
measuring, and concept of length, 117
membership of a class, 12, 26
memory, Hume, 86
Menninger, Karl, 117n
Meno (Plato), 12, 34–43
Metaphysics (Aristotle), 16, 32, 61, 74
mind, as cause of everything, 14
miracle, 53
mistake, language and, 124, 132–3
monad, and Plato's theory of forms,
  23, 24
Moore, G. E., 82
  on knowing, 125–7, 129, 132

moral character, choice and,
  69–71
Moral Science Club, 122
moral virtue, Aristotle, 76
morals, Hume's theory of foundation
  of, 119
Movement of Animals (Aristotle), 73, 74
mystery, 122–3

name,
  early theory of forms, 9
  and function, 108–10
  non-substitutability of, viii, ix
  and revised theory of forms, 25
necessity,
  Aristotle, 49, 52–3, 54, 56
  de dicto, 82, 84
  de re, 82, 84
  language and, 118, 120, 121–2
  and truth, 81–5
negatibility, 108, 111
negation, x, 4
  Aristotle, 44, 45–9
  and matter, 58
  Plato's revised theory of forms, 21,
    30–31
  of predicate, 108–9
Neo-Scholastics, 57
Neurath, 92
Newman, Cardinal, 53
Nicomachean Ethics (Aristotle), 48, 73,
  74, 75, 76, 102
'no new information' thesis, 123
non-being, in revised theory of forms,
  29–30
non-existence,
  Aristotle, 48, 49
  Parmenides, 4
nothingness of what-is-not, vii
noun, self-predication, 22
nourishment, 64
number,
  and early theory of forms, 16–20
  language and, 116–18
  unit as matter of, 59
Number Words and Number Symbols
  (Menninger), 117n

object, xi

object—*cont.*
  concept and, 108–9
  early theory of forms, 12
  Wittgenstein, 108–11
'objects of knowledge', 83
'objects of opinion', 83
obligation, language and, 119
On Certainty (Wittgenstein), 89n, 124n, 125, 126, 130
one,
  form of the, ix–x, 21, 22–8, 30
  non-identity of, viii
opinion, irrational true, 38
'other', Plato's revised theory of forms, 22, 30–31

Parmenides, vii–xi
  early theory of forms, 10, 13, 20
  on what cannot be thought, 3–8
  revised theory of forms, 24–5, 28, 32
Parmenides (Plato), ix
  revised theory of forms, 21–3, 25–6, 28–30, 32–3
part, Plato's revised theory of forms, 21, 26–8, 30–31
participation,
  early theory of forms, 9, 10, 12, 13
  revised theory of forms, 29, 31, 32
passion, will as, 101, 102
past time reference, 49, 52–3, 56
perception,
  and belief, 87
  early theory of forms, 9
  language and, 121
  understanding and, 36
persuasion, language and, 128, 131, 132
Phaedo (Plato), 9, 10, 13, 15, 16–20
  revised theory of forms, 21, 22, 23
Phaedrus (Plato), 9, 10
Philebus (Plato), 23, 24
Philosophical Investigations (Wittgenstein), 23, 112
Philosophische Bemerkungen (Wittgenstein), 89
physics, Wittgenstein, 127–9
Physics (Aristotle), 50, 58, 59
'picture of the world', Wittgenstein, 128–30, 130n, 131

place,
  and beginning of existence, 95
  definition by means of, 63
'place-matter', 59
Plato, vii, ix, x–xi
  and Aristotle, 72
  early theory of forms, 9–13, 15–20
  knowledge, 81, 83
  language, 112, 113
  revised theory of forms, 21–7, 29–32
Platonic theory of forms, 9–20, 116, 124
Plato's Philosophy of Mathematics (Wedberg), 12
pleasure, 107
  positive attitude, 102–3
Pompey, 91, 92
Popper, Karl, 64–5
potentiality, Aristotle's notion of, 48
practical reasoning, Aristotle, 72–5
practice, transition of rules to, 121
predicates, Wittgenstein, 108–10
predication,
  and assertion, xi, 100
  contradictory, 28–9, 32
  copula of, 29
  self, 11, 22
  ultimate subject of, 57
prediction, 53, 54
present time reference, 49, 52–3
principles, 15, 19
private ostensive definition, 13
probability, Aristotle, 49
prognosis, Hume, 86
promises,
  language and, 118–20
  'natural unintelligibility' of, 118–19, 120–21
proof-syllogism, 73, 74
proofs,
  Aristotle, 73
  Hume, 93
  understanding, 34–43
properties, non-existent, 4
property-variable, 5
prophecy, 53
proposition,
  general theory of positive/negative, 103

proposition—*cont.*
  negated, 31, 44
Psychologie vom empirischen Standpunkt
    (Brentano), 100
psycho-somatic sensation, 104

quality, notions, of, 98
quantity, notions of, 98
Quine, W. V. O., 5, 11, 12, 28, 50

Ramsey, F. P., 108–11
rationality, in religion, 122
realism, and empiricism, 115, 133
reality, language and, xi, 113
reason,
  and conviction, 127
  Hume, 75
  and persuasion, 131
record, chain of, 88, 89
relations, 13
religion, 130n
  Wittgenstein, 122–3
Republic (Plato), 9, 10, 11, 16–20, 23, 25
resemblance, 10
rights, language and, 118
Rivo, Peter de, 54
Road Belong Cargo (Lawrence), 126n
rules, language and, 118, 120–22, 128,
    131
Russell, Bertrand, 109

same, Plato's revised theory of forms,
    21, 22, 24, 29, 30
sameness, language and, 114
science, language and, 125
self-predication, *see* predication
sensation, language and, 115
separate existence, doctrine of, 11, 13
separation, early theory of forms, 16
set-theory, 13
Set Theory and its Logic (Quine), 11
sight, and colour, 40–43
similarity, Plato, 10–11
simplicity, belief and, 129–30
Simplicius, 30
Sixtus IV, Pope, 54
Socrates, 108
  early theory of forms, 10–16, 19–20,
    23, 28

Meno, 34–43
'something', cf. 'one thing', 23
Sophist (Plato), ix, 12
  revised theory of forms, 21–7,
    29–30, 33
Sophists, vii, 15
soul,
  pre-existence of, 15
  understanding proofs, 34–5, 41–3
space, and beginning of existence,
    94–5
spatio-temporal continuity, 88–9
Spinoza, Baruch, ix
starting-point, 87
Stenius, Erik, 108–10
Stoics, 44
Studies in Plato's Metaphysics (ed.
    Allen), 22n
'stuff', and matter, 59–60
'subject-predicate proposition', 109
substance,
  matter and, 59, 61, 63
  theory of, xi
substitution, and revised theory of
    forms, 25
suffusion, Brentano's metaphor of, 106
Summa Theologica (Aquinas), 74, 81
superstition, 124, 125
syllogism, 73, 74
symmetry, belief and, 129–30

Tarski, 13
teaching,
  knowledge and, 90
  understanding and, 42
Theaetetus, 29–30, 31, 32
Theaetetus (Plato), 28, 33, 50
theology, 123
thought, xi
  Aquinas, 83
  Aristotle, 75
  characterization of, 85
  Parmenides, vii, x, 3–8
time,
  beginning of existence, 94–5
  definition by means of, 63
totality, cf. whole, 28
Tractatus Logico-Philosophicus
    (Wittgenstein), xi, 54, 108–11

'transcendentals', doctrine of, 22
Treatise of Human Nature, A (Hume),
   86, 93, 121n
truth,
  Aristotle, 44–7, 49, 50–55, 56
  Hume, 93
  necessity and, 81–5
  objective, 127
  'practical', 66, 76–7
  understanding, 34, 39, 41–2
truth-condition, 51
truth-functional expression, 50
truth-possibilities, 51
truth-table, 53, 54
truth value, 30, 50
type, theory of, 9–12; *see also* forms

understanding, philosophic, 84
understanding proofs, 34–43
unexceptionable, how to use, 56
unit, matter of number, 59
unity, and Plato's theory of forms, 24
universals,
  Aristotle, 44, 47
  Wittgenstein, 108–11
unthinkability of what-is-not, vii

variables, reference of, 5
volume, and matter, 58
voluntary act, Brentano, 105

Wedberg, Anders, 12
'whichever happens', Aristotle, 47, 48
Whitehead, A. N., xi
whole, Plato's revised theory of
   forms, 21, 22, 26, 28
will,
  Aristotle, 66–70, 75–6
  and emotion, 100–107
  freedom of, 54
Wittgenstein, Ludwig, xi, 13, 23,
   89–90
  and Aristotle, 54
  linguistic idealism, 112–33
  Tractatus, 108–11
word, linguistic idealism, 112–13,
   116–17
Word and Object (Quine), 28n

Xenophon, 90

Zettel (Wittgenstein), 113

Printed in Poland
by Amazon Fulfillment
Poland Sp. z o.o., Wrocław
27 November 2020

16bbe1d1-413d-4ced-a875-5c6ffeda988dR01